Shadows

Shadows

An Album of the Irish People
1841 – 1914

Michael O'Connell

THE O'BRIEN PRESS

RTE

First published 1985 by The O'Brien Press Ltd.
20 Victoria Road, Dublin 6.
in association with
Radio Telefis Eireann (RTE)
© Copyright reserved.

British Library Cataloguing in Publication Data
O'Connell, Michael
Shadows An Album of the Irish People 1841–1914.
1. Ireland – Social life and customs – 19th century – Pictorial works.
2. Ireland – Social life and customs – 20th century – Pictorial works.
1. Title
941.5081′022′2 –DA950,1

ISBN 0-86278-101-9.

10 9 8 7 6 5 4 3 2 1

Book design and layout: Michael O'Brien and Debby Bell
Editing: Íde ní Laoghaire and Phyllis Burgess
Cover design: Frank Spiers
Front cover photo: John Cooney, RTE Guide
Typesetting: Design and Art Facilities
Origination: Redsetter Ltd.
Halftones: Irish Photo Ltd.
Cover separations: Litho Studios
Printing: Irish Elsevier, Shannon

Page 1: A cycle-rail inspection team trundle along near Whitehead, County Antrim.

Page 2: Work as a shop assistant became an expanding option as a career in the early days of this century for both men and, less generally, women. The assistant had to pay a fee and serve an apprenticeship to the shopowner.

Page 3: Comparative affluence in the social pecking order of the west of Ireland: this woman owns a donkey rather than having to haul the burden herself.

Page 6: The tenement children of Dublin were described as 'That characteristic Dublin figure, the street child with its tousled head, its bare legs and the quaintly fluttering rags of its wardrobe'.

Contents

Introduction   7

Chapter 1 – The West   14

Chapter 2 – The Big House   28

Chapter 3 – Women   40

Chapter 4 – The Catholic Church   52

Chapter 5 – The Dublin Slums   62

Chapter 6 – Fashion   74

Chapter 7 – Children   86

Chapter 8 – Sport   100

Chapter 9 – The Empire   110

Chapter 10 – Behind the Camera   122

Illustration Sources   132

For my wife
Mary Donovan
without whose arduous work and
loving support this book would have
been impossible.

Introduction

Michael O'Connell

When I first started my quest for old photographs while making the *Shadows* series for RTE, I was mainly interested in photographs which would tell me something of the social history of Ireland from the earliest days of photography until the Great War. Television had already adequately treated political events and the available political photographs. However, my interest lay in photographs of a social nature and the clues they give us of the lives led by the men, women, children who went before us.

Any lingering romantic notions I may have entertained of life in Ireland before the turn of the century were dispelled by the time I had viewed in excess of 200,000 photographs and glass negatives. While there was undoubted excitement during the search, I was continually faced with the stark reality of grim deprivation faced by our former generations. The photographs serve to clear the fog of myth and reveal the truth.

Unfortunately, this truth may not be available to those of future years who wish to chronicle 200 years of Irish photographs. Unless a National Photographic Archive is established urgently, where these gems of our heritage are preserved under rigorously controlled conditions, our descendants will be unable to share in that sense of privilege and excitement which attended my search. The present custodians of our photographic history, both private and public, care for their collections with love and diligence but it is only in a national archive that they can be given optimum conditions for survival.

At the outset of my long search into our photographic past, two people in particular helped steer me in directions other than the obvious: Peter Walsh, curator of the Guinness Museum gave freely of his expertise and time as did Eddie Chandler who is probably Ireland's foremost expert on early Victorian photography. In Northern Ireland, Brian Mercer Walker generously shared his research with me and I owe him a large debt of gratitude.

My assistant in RTE, Jill Healy, ably and unsparingly accompanied me during twelve months' research and helped me in the final selection of the 12,000 photographs for the series. We followed many false trails, but the fine photographic collections we did unearth were sufficient compensation. I am very grateful to all the officers of the various institutions we visited who facilitated our work. A large debt of gratitude is owed particularly to those private collectors who invited us into their homes and allowed access to their photographs.

While the photographs did indeed tell their stories, they did not provide a comprehensive social history and I am deeply indebted to Dr Mary Daly of UCD for the amount of research work, assistance and patience she gave so generously. Her contribution to both the series and this book has been enormous. I am very grateful also to Michael Ryan of RTE for the supreme efforts and dedicated professionalism which he brought to the writing of his superb scripts for the series. The evocative music by Jim Doherty and the creative sensitivity of Maurice Brennan contributed enormously to the overall impact of *Shadows*.

Not many Controllers of Programmes would have had the vision to allow a producer the scope to undertake such an enterprise as *Shadows*. Muiris Mac Conghail did, and I thank him. Deirdre Gahan deserves my thanks for cheerfully labouring through the typing of the manuscript and Íde ní Laoghaire and Michael O'Brien of The O'Brien Press gave support and guidance in bringing this book to fruition.

Finally, thanks to Deirdre and Fergal, my children. They are a constant reminder to me of the future and the photographic legacy which is their right.

Opposite: Reception for the Dublin Fusiliers on their return from the Boer War in South Africa, 1902, at the RDS, Ballsbridge, Dublin.

Above: Harvest celebration, Toome, County Antrim. Taken by William Greene, a professional photographer from the North of Ireland.

Page 10: The members of a Donegal clachan, or community, gathered together. Apart from providing essential help to each other in farm work, neighbours socialised together at night – story-telling, gossiping and singing.

Page 11: Coopers at work at the Guinness Brewery, St. James's Gate.

1860 – 1910
The changing face of Ireland's premier thoroughfare

Above: A very narrow Carlisle Bridge looking towards Sackville Street in 1860. Note the semaphore on the roof of the GPO used to transmit messages prior to the arrival of the telegraph. The ladies still wear crinolines, while the gentlemen sport stovepipe hats. Gas lamps light the street, while traffic is still disorderly – driving on the left-hand side had yet to be introduced.

Right: Carlisle Bridge in 1873. Horse-drawn omnibuses had arrived, but there was still room for a flock of sheep to be driven across the bridge. Several omnibus companies provided transport to the suburbs.

Left: The statue of Daniel O'Connell now dominates the scene at a widened O'Connell Bridge in the 1880s. Public subscription was used to fund the building of the statue, the foundation stone having been laid in 1875. Between the O'Connell Monument and Nelson Pillar stands the memorial to John Gray, who provided Dublin with its water supply, erected in 1870.

Right: O'Connell Bridge 1910 – now crisscrossed with overhead cables, marking the introduction of the electric trams for the Dublin Tramway Co. which had been introduced in 1896. The building on the right with the small canopy roof was probably one of the shortest-lived buildings in Dublin. Built in 1901, it was to be destroyed during the 1916 Rising.

SACKVILLE St. DUBLIN. 2919. W.L.

CHAPTER ONE

The West

The famine of the 1840s lives in Irish folk memory to the present day. However it is less well known that the people of the west of Ireland were victims of many minor famines for the remainder of the nineteenth century and indeed even into the early days of the Free State. Combined with gruelling poverty, the reality of life for those in the west was so harsh as to be almost beyond our understanding – had we not photographs to remind us. Not only potato blight subscribed to the poverty of the people of the west; the system of farming used equally caused suffering. Known as the Rundale system, each farmer divided up his farm among his children, each child inheriting upon marriage. For example, a thirty-acre farm, divided amongst one generation of six children reduced this holding to a size which could hardly be expected to sustain new families, let alone the succeeding generation. Also to be fair-minded, the land was not allocated in tidy packages but divided so as to give all an equal share of bog, rock, marsh and, where it existed, fertile soil.

Thus a young couple beginning their marriage with perhaps ten acres, might find it scattered into as many as fifty different lots. Their new house built of stone in only two days was situated beside the neighbours in the 'clachan' or village. The central point of the home was the hearth, complete with crane and hook holding the pots and kettle for cooking. Around the fire were three-legged stools and perhaps a bench. In such homes housework as we know it did not exist: there were no beds to make – a pile of straw on the floor sufficed for sleeping; there were no windows to be cleaned nor furniture to be polished. Only later did flagstones replace earth as the floor covering. The interiors were dark and dank and animals were brought into the house at night to protect them from foxes. The resulting manure was not cleaned away, a drain in the middle of the floor keeping the animals in their own quarters, and this, in effect, made animal housing an integral part of human housing.

The relentless struggle with the land made the appalling living conditions of the family pale into insignificance. It was impossible to make a living from such land in such small scattered holdings, but the fight went on nonetheless. So enormous was the task that all in the family were

involved – men, women, children, grandparents alike; if any distinction was made it was that the women carried the heaviest burden in every way. Crops, usually potatoes, were sown nearest the house, and cattle and sheep were grazed in the outfields. Land near the sea could be fertilised by seaweed, otherwise it was useless for tilling. As fields were so small, machinery could not be accommodated, and was far too expensive in any case. Ploughs were unknown; sickles rather than scythes were used for reaping as they were more manageable for women. Threshing too was done by hand, two women being needed to tediously grind corn with a quern.

Farming, then, was done the primitive, the manual, the *poor* way. Any cash income derived from such subsistence living was almost miraculous. The sample budgets below of two families of the west show how impossible was the struggle.

Sample family budget: Dunfanaghy, Co. Donegal. Number in family 10, arable land 4 acres, rent £2 16s. 6d.

Value of produce:	Living expenses:
potatoes 1 acre £4 0s. 0d.	rent £2 16s. 6d.
turnips 1 rood £1 0s. 0d.	food 14s. 8d. per week;
oats 2 acres,	£38 2s. 8d. per year
3 roods £10 15s. 0d.	clothing £14 0s. 0d.
profit on stock £2 10s. 0d.	
total income £18 5s. 0d.	total expenditure £54 19s. 2d.
	deficit £36 14s. 2d.

This family got only one-third income from the land and had to struggle to make the rest elsewhere.

These tables show that some of our preconceived ideas about life in traditional Ireland ought to be re-examined. Our folk history is that of a poor peasant farmer paying exorbitant rent to a greedy, absentee landlord. However absent the landlord, or poor the farmer, the figures above reveal that the amount paid by these families to the landlord was hardly extortionist. The accusation of extortion could in fact be levied more against the local shopkeeper who sometimes charged 15 per cent interest for the credit advanced to families during hard times, while the bank rate stood at 3 per cent.

Interestingly, also, the tables show that the poor Aran family spent no money on clothes during the year. Traditionally, families were self-sufficient in clothing, their own sheep providing wool which was spun and dyed by the women. Only later in the century were boots common – for men. Indeed it is obvious from the budgets that footwear must have been a luxury.

Sample budget: Aran Islands (poor family).

Income from sale:	Expenses:
2 pigs £4 0s. 0d.	rent £1 10s. 0d.
sheep £2 0s. 0d.	church dues 5s. 0d.
one calf £4 0s. 0d.	meal and flour £9 10s. 0d.
kelp £9 0s. 0d. (kelp is critical here)	groceries £3 10s. 0d.
	tobacco £2 12s. 0d.
seaweed £1 0s. 0d.	turf £3 4s. 0d. (no bogs on Aran)
eggs £1 0s. 0d.	extras £1 0s. 0d.
total income £21 0s. 0d.	total expenditure £21 11s. 0d.

The Royal Commission on Congestion in Ireland. 2nd report, Appendix 4; 'Typical Family'. 1907.

CURING HERRINGS, ARDGLASS.

Opposite: Prior to the intervention of the Congested Districts Board, boats in the west were tiny and could only fish close to shore. The board subsidised the purchase of large boats built in Arklow and sailed them around to the west. These boats could fish the larger shoals farther from the shore and with the use of nets, provide catches large enough to sustain a fishing industry. The arrival of the railways meant ready access to the Dublin and London markets.

Above: Kelp seaweed was harvested in the late spring by wading thigh-deep into a cold sea. To help people rise above subsistence level, the Congested Districts Board made strong efforts to develop the kelp industry in order to generate much needed cash. The skills needed to teach were imported from the west of Scotland.

Right: Premature ageing came from the gruelling battle with an unyielding land.

Facing such an endless cycle of debt, credit and poverty, the solutions open to the people of the west were drastic. Men and teenage girls went to Scotland, often for six months of the year, to work, leaving wives and remaining children to cope as best they could. More heartbreaking were the hiring fairs where more prosperous farmers engaged children from eight years of age for periods of about six months at a time.

It was realised that piecemeal attempts to solve the problems of the west would be totally inadequate. The government then decided to undertake a radically innovative and widespread programme of intervention.

In 1891, the Congested Districts Board was established, its first task being to compile a report on the facts of the ills which continued to plague the west. The crazy patchwork allocation of tracts of land under the Rundale system had to be tackled, however monumental a task it may have seemed initially. Entire estates were purchased from landlords and were reallocated to local farmers in the form of more

Opposite top: A creel of turf is carried home. While the saving of turf was back-breaking and time-consuming it at least provided free fuel.

Opposite bottom: In its efforts to inject cash into the west the Congested Districts Board relied on the traditional relief scheme of road building. Wages were a shilling a day with food included or one and sixpence a day without food.

Right: Social ranking in the west of Ireland.

recognisable farms such as we know today. Apart from the obvious economic impact of such a large scheme, one important social implication was, perhaps, overlooked by its designers. Previously, as we have seen, all local houses were huddled together in a clachan. Such an arrangement gave rise to the traditional neighbourliness and hospitality of the west. People gathered in each other's houses for singing, story-telling and conversation. Neighbours helped build houses, shared equipment and supported each other when times were hard. Now, the Congested Districts Board was to provide a house for each family, located on its own newly designated farm often at a great distance from old neighbours and family. Thus was born the isolation and loneliness now more often associated with the west.

The Congested Districts Board had many objectives in establishing road building schemes. The entire area needed an injection of cash and road building was intended as a relief scheme to provide money for the poorer families who were to build them. Prior to this it had not been possible to transport superfluous produce from the isolated communities to larger markets as many areas were inaccessible to wheeled vehicles.

The Board hoped that, as a result of its efforts in agriculture, fishing and cottage industries, the west would soon have much superfluous produce to 'export' and thus end the subsistence life which had been its lot for so long. To improve the standard of agriculture in the west was one of the Board's first priorities, and, indeed, there was much room for improvement. Travelling instructors supplied seed potatoes and taught farmers the benefit of spraying the potato crop to protect against blight. Attempts were made also to educate people in the value of crop rotation for an exhausted soil. Improved animal breeding was introduced in the form of bulls and horses at stud. Better laying hens and ducks were introduced and the Board tried to speed up the process of supplying eggs to the English market; previously, the system operated by the local shopkeeper often took six weeks from Connemara hen to English breakfast table! On the whole, it is doubtful that the Board's plans for agriculture in the west were of much value. Similarly we cannot tell if the peasant farmers' natural conservatism hindered them from being receptive to the new and strange plans of the Board's itinerant instructor.

Left: Bound for Sunday Mass, having achieved the pinnacle of success in the west, ownership of a horse.

Above: Most industry in the west was domestic. An exception was the Killybegs Carpet Factory established by the Hon. Frederick Wrench, a member of the Congested Districts Board, and Alexander Morton, a Scottish carpet manufacturer. They set up a factory at Killybegs and subsequently extended their operations to factories in Kilcar, Annagry and Crolly. By World War One each employed 200 workers in hand-crafted Donegal wool carpets.

Opposite: The Congested Districts Board brought lace-making classes to the west. Unfortunately the responsibility for selling the lace was left to the teachers who had few marketing skills; the project had little success.

Fishing techniques off the west coast were perhaps almost as primitive as those used in agriculture. The only vessels used were currachs and the equipment consisted solely of a hook and line. Thus, when the herrings move out to sea from the coast off Erris, the prosperous fishing industry there declined because the currachs were unable to follow. Although in most areas fishing was worth less than £5 per annum to a family, it was obvious to the Congested Districts Board that fishing was an area which was ripe for development. Money was provided to buy boats, and Scottish instructors employed to train the men in their use. Mackerel fishing was introduced off the west coast using boats brought from Arklow. Nets and other equipment could now be bought by the fishermen with the help of low interest loans from the Board. Supplies of ice were also provided by the Board to preserve the fish on its journey to market on the newly built railways. Altogether, the benefits of the Board's interventions in fishing were more obvious than in agriculture. A fishing industry was established by them and was flourishing in Donegal, Galway, Kerry and Cork by the eve of the First World War.

Having intervened to enhance the life of the fisherman and farmer, the Board was also anxious to improve the economic position of women in the west of Ireland. The bog roads built by the Board certainly eased the task of bringing home the turf, a job usually done by the women who carried it over rough terrain in creels on their backs. The Board felt that cash in these women's hands would be

wisely used and decided that efforts should be made to capitalise on indigenous crafts and skills, such as spinning and knitting. Such skills were weakest in Mayo and Galway, and therefore the Board introduced teachers here to pass on embroidery and needlework skills to local women. Seventy-six lace schools were established, the most effective teachers of course being those who could speak Irish. As with the fishing industry, cottage industries also needed help to develop the market for the resulting products. Exhibitions of the women's work were arranged, not only by the Congested Districts Board, but also by the Department of Agriculture and by individuals such as Lady Aberdeen, the wife of the viceroy, in the hope of bringing the crafts to the attention of wealthier families in Dublin

Left: A Donegal rundale community clinging to the western seaboard in the late 1870s. Despite poverty there was a good sense of community; most people were related to their neighbours.

Above: Fair Day. The produce of a year's labour was sold here but it never gave enough profit to pay off the debts to landlords, the church and the shopkeeper.

and London. In the main, however, the marketing of the finished products was the responsibility of the local teacher. Since these teachers had been recruited from the genteel middle classes, their skills in marketing were few, if any. This, combined with the low return for labour – a woman doing almost nothing else would earn £5 per annum – meant that the domestic crafts schemes of the Board did not flourish.

Whatever money was earned was often used to send a member of the family to the United States to join previous emigrants. Their letters home, and the arrival of tourists for the first time on the new roads and railways, spoke of a different life, a life where hunger and abject poverty was almost unknown. The congested districts were soon to be no longer that – they would be drained of people until they became desolate and deserted. The Congested Districts Board had, however nobly intentioned, provided too little, too amateurishly and much too late.

Top left: Although the women are barefooted the impact of the Congested Districts Board can be seen in the white-washed houses, better clothes and general prosperity.

Left: The arrival of the tourist highlighted harsh contrasts between two worlds.

Opposite: The run-down towns of the west were purely market centres, there were no industries to generate wealth or create employment.

CHAPTER TWO

The Big House

When Queen Victoria ascended the throne in 1837, life for the Dillon family at Clonbrock Castle was proceeding with the even tenor which had marked it throughout the centuries. Sir Henry De Leon, who had accompanied the Earl of Morton, later to be King John, to Ireland in 1185, had been granted tracts of land in Longford and Westmeath. A descendant of his, Thomas Dillon who was Commissioner for Connacht in 1576, bought Clonbrock and the family continued to live there until this century. At the time of Victoria's coronation, Luke Dillon, the second Lord Clonbrock was master at Clonbrock. His wife Anastasia died in 1816. Their eldest son, Robert, had been sent to be educated first at a private preparatory school in England at the age of eight, as was the custom among landed gentry in Ireland. Eton and Oxford followed, and while there he often visited the home of his father's friend, Lord Francis Spencer, later Lord Churchill, at his home near Blenheim. When Robert married Caroline Spencer in 1830 a bonfire was lit on top of Clonbrock Castle to celebrate the union of both families.

Caroline and Robert settled in Clonbrock and between 1831 and 1848 had twelve children. Only two sons survived to adulthood, Robert Villiers and Luke Gerald, but their seven daughters lived to old age. Famine came to the tenants of Clonbrock in 1846 and in his efforts to help, Robert had all the deer in Clonbrock's deerpark shot and distributed as food. All hounds and horses on the estate were also sold. This response was fairly typical of resident landlords at the time and the image of the heartless landlord evicting his unfortunate tenant can be viewed largely as myth. Indeed one of the Mahons of Castlegar, a neighbouring family, was often to be seen slipping rent money back under his tenants' doors. Evictions were rare and rents seldom increased, with both landlord and tenant adopting a live-and-let-live attitude. The peak of land agitation was not to come until the late 1870s and 1880s when agricultural prices fell so sharply that rents which had been easy to pay a few years previously, became impossible.

In the meantime however, a relative peace reigned. Luke Gerald, oldest surviving son of Robert and Caroline had come of age, a large party being held for family friends and tenants to celebrate the event. Gerald himself was absent,

having been employed by the Diplomatic Service after leaving Oxford. He retired from the service to be near his mother in her last illness and while living at home explored the new hobby of photography with his sister Georgina. At the same time he was a frequent visitor to Mote where Augusta Crofton shared his photographic interest. So much so, that when Gerald announced to his father that he was going to propose to Augusta, Robert responded 'Pooh, pooh. You only want to photograph together.' Nevertheless Augusta and Gerald married two months later. Great excitement was generated in the district by the wedding; Clonbrock tenants presented Gerald with three tall silver centrepieces, while Lord Crofton subscribed £100 for Augusta to spend on jewellery while in London buying her wedding dress.

The young couple began their married life in the Phoenix Park in Dublin where Gerald had been appointed Private Secretary to the Lord Lieutenant. They lived there

Previous page: Croquet party at Clonbrock c.1865. Apart from the large resident family, visitors came frequently, with their servants.

Above: Butterfly netting party at Clonbrock. Augusta's relatives from left: Hon. Elizabeth Dillon, Hon. Edward Crofton, Hon. Katherine Dillon, Hon. Georgina Dillon and Hon. Robert Dillon – Gerald's brothers and sisters.

Right: Augusta, Lady Clonbrock, interviews a tenant. When she and Gerald celebrated their Golden Wedding anniversary in 1916 the servants and employees presented them with a beautiful gold cup.

Opposite: The photographic studio built by Augusta and Gerald in 1869. Augusta recorded in her diary on June 4th 'Agreed with Maghton to build the Photograph House for £10'. This sum paid for labour, all materials being supplied.

Sir Robert Peel at a Clonbrock shooting party, December 1863 – standing directly in front of the pillar between the crinolined Augusta Congreve and Caroline Dillon. The photograph was taken by Gerald. The party had bagged 45 woodcock and 36 pheasant.

for two years until the defeat of the Tory Government terminated Gerald's appointment. It was to a very crowded Clonbrock that the new family returned in 1868 as all of Gerald's sisters still lived at home. Although it is not referred to in the family's history, it is possible that the family could not afford to dowry so many daughters. Certainly the Mahon family at Castlegar who were also well endowed with daughters had one who bewailed her misfortune when at 18 she was still in the schoolroom, the family being unable to afford the inevitable consequences of her coming out. Whatever the reason, Augusta settled down to raise her four children in the company of her husband's large family.

Mealtimes were an important ritual at Clonbrock, and the family dined well. Breakfast consisted of porridge, boiled eggs, brown and white scones and toast, while on a side table stood cold sirloin of beef, ham, pressed beef and a cold pie. Beer was drunk with lunch, which included meat, pudding and plum and ginger cake. Tea was an informal affair, taken in the drawing room with bread and butter balanced on saucers. Most important of all meals was dinner eaten at 7.45 p.m. having been formally announced by the valet. Soup or fish began the meal while the main course had a choice of two meats. Cheese, dessert and a glass of port concluded the meal, the ladies withdrawing at this stage often not to be rejoined by the men until 10 p.m.

A large retinue of servants was required to maintain such a household and at least fifteen worked indoors headed by Mrs Dent, the housekeeper. She took charge of the cake and jam-making and had responsibility for all the towels and linens of the house. A tall gaunt woman dressed in grey for mornings and black for afternoons, she presided over the servants' meals, after dinner leading the upper echelons of the servants into her own quarters to take dessert. The servants' spiritual welfare was certainly not neglected at Clonbrock; seats were arranged to take those who wanted to go to church, while Mrs Dent herself walked to give an underservant her seat and so save the girl's shoes. A family prayer service was held each morning, the servants filing in in strict hierarchical order. Gerald's sister Frances held a Bible class for the servant girls in her room every Sunday at 6 p.m. and all are reported to have attended and enjoyed it.

Augusta's and Robert's children meanwhile were often closer to the life of the servants of the house than to that of the adults. They often took tea with Mrs Dent and the upper servants and were especially close to Mamy their nurse. The servants' concerns were theirs and they commiserated with each other whenever scolded. Their father never visited the nursery and it was Mamy who constantly read stories, made clothes for their dolls and who

accompanied them on outings. Augusta they saw at stated times; she heard their prayers each morning before breakfast, sat with them for a little after lunch and spent the usual 'children's hour' with them after tea.

Life must have been awkward for Augusta at Clonbrock. While Gerald's father was living she was not mistress of the house and was anxious lest her sisters-in-law would find the children a nuisance. Less extrovert than the Dillons, she and Gerald built a photographic studio in the grounds of Clonbrock where they could pursue their hobby at which Augusta, particularly excelled. When staying in Dublin she helped found the Irish Distressed Ladies' Society and worked hard at its headquarters in Rutland Square. On the estate, she started the Clonbrock and Castlegar Co-operative Poultry Society in 1898 to help local women obtain reasonable prices for their eggs. At the outbreak of

Gerald, Lord Clonbrock, (left) supervising farm work with W. Hay, the steward. He continued the tradition of his father Robert of whom it was said 'There is not a detail connected with his property about which his interest is not as keen, his judgement not as clever and his benevolent feelings not as strong as they have ever been.'

the Boer War she collected woollens, cigarettes and other comfort items for the troops. Two national schools had been established on the estate by Robert, the teachers being selected and paid by him. Augusta took a special interest in the schools, visiting them often and awarding prizes for attendance and needlework. The latter consisted mostly of baby clothes for which she had provided the material. Afterwards the clothes were given to needy tenants by the tenants' maternity nurse who was employed by Augusta.

A staunch Unionist, Gerald had many administrative duties in County Galway. The meetings he attended included those of the Assizes, the Petty and Road sessions, the Board of Guardians, the Dispensary, Lunatic Asylum Board, the Parish Vestry and the Diocesan Synod and Council. Trips to Dublin were made to attend the Church Representative Body and General Synod meetings. For relaxation he fished in summer and shot in winter. His grandfather, Luke, had planted extensive woods in the early years of the century and these remained dear to Gerald. He spent many hours supervising the forester and woodmen in the maintenance and further planting of the woods.

When his father died in December 1893 and Gerald

Opposite: Branding sheep on the Clonbrock estate – note the 'C' in the labourer's hand.

Left: Martin, a gardener, with a box of begonias for the front hall at Clonbrock in 1901, grown in what had been the orchid house. During the time of 'figures, plans and poverty' all the orchids had been sold to Lord Ardilaun. Sir Robert Dillon, an orchid lover, had hated surrendering them.

Below: Consultation with a gardener. Although all Gerald's sisters loved to grow things the garden was strictly the preserve of the staff; the ladies contented themselves with window boxes.

succeeded to the title of fourth Baron Clonbrock, his life remained almost unchanged apart from visits to London to attend the House of Lords. At Clonbrock, however, life was to change fundamentally and domestically due to the radical land reforms which were to sweep the country. With their father dead, Gerald's sisters could no longer consider Clonbrock their home, and in March 1894 they left to live in England. Augusta recorded in her diary that day, 'So ends the second volume of my life.' She had come into her own and was mistress of Clonbrock. The house would never be the same again and many of the servants who had postponed retirement began to leave.

Politically too, change was occurring. The Land Act of 1881 had introduced government-controlled rents and this in effect sounded the death knell for Irish landlordism. Prices continued to fall however, so that rents were again too high and in the mid-1880s the Plan of Campaign was

Left: A poultry show held by the Clonbrock and Castlegar Co-operative Society, founded by Lady Augusta Dillon.

Above: Hon. Katherine Dillon visiting a tenant family. When she moved to Lemington to what she described as 'this horrid towny life' she continued her philanthropic work, being allocated a district by the rector to visit.

Opposite: Gerald and Augusta Dillons' daughters, Georgina, Edith and Ethel. When she was seven 'Georgy' contracted polio and was lame all her life although able to cycle a tricycle and ride. Neither Georgina nor Ethel married. Ethel, in 1915, was a nurse in Bermondsey military hospital, returning home to care for Gerald in his last illness in 1917.

Opposite: Edith's wedding in 1905 to Sir William Mahon of Castlegar, the ceremony performed by the Bishop of Killaloe. A London firm in their estimate for the wedding cake included the cost of two men to deliver it to ensure its safe arrival. Augusta concluded that a cake from Dublin would have to suffice!

Above: The honeymooners return to Castlegar. As was customary, the tenants detached the horses at the village and dragged the carriage for the remainder of the journey.

begun to demand even further rent reductions. Rents from the Clonbrock tenants began to be erratically paid and in 1886 plans to cope with a reduced standard of living were made. Five servants were made redundant, the event being noted in the family diary as 'The first fruits of Parnell & Co.' Reductions were made in the stables, wood, farm and garden. Then in 1913, under the Irish Land Purchase Act the entire estate excluding the house was sold; there were to be no more tenants to be attended to, no more rent offices and no more agents to administer.

Gerald died in 1917 and Augusta in 1928. Their only son Robert Edward remained at Clonbrock House and never married. In 1976 the entire contents of the house were auctioned by Christies of London. An era had ended, not only for the family, but Ireland.

The source of this chapter is: Edith Mahon (née Dillon). 'The Dillons of Clonbrock'. MS, The National Library, Dublin.

CHAPTER THREE

Women

While the suffragettes of the early twentieth century were agitating for votes for women and for a say in the running of their country, vast numbers of women were already shouldering the entire responsibility of life at a day-to-day level. To them fell the task of wage-earning for the family and also the clothing, feeding and rearing of the next generation.

Their geographical location in Ireland, however, as well as their class, determined how they lived, and important differences emerge when we examine the lives of women of different corners of Ireland.

One of the biggest differences between families of unskilled labourers in Belfast and Dublin was that in Belfast job opportunities for women abounded. At the turn of the century the linen industry was a domestic one, the work being done by both men and women at home. The industrial revolution had a social aspect as well, and the gradual opening of mills and factories saw the heavier dirtier jobs there being allocated to men, while women still retained their part of the process in skilled jobs such as spinning and weaving. Families which enjoyed decent housing and adequate meals were one of the rewards reaped by Ulster women's skills and access to work.

Within their work, however, there were strict class distinctions. Women who worked in the weaving factories felt superior to the 'shawlies' of the spinning mills. While a weaver's work was cleaner and somehow more individualistic, the mill women worked a wet process and had to wear protective aprons and work barefooted. Their wages differed somewhat too, but their contribution to the family budget of ten to fourteen shillings a week would have seemed a princely sum to working women elsewhere in Ireland. The wages earned by the women of Derry's shirt factories, for example, might be their families' entire income, husbands not being fortunate enough to have access to the industry enjoyed by Belfast.

Not all married women in Belfast worked outside the home, however. Those whose husbands held a craft job in the shipyards, for example, worked in the home and we read contemporary accounts of their prodigious housework.

AN IRISH HARVESTERS DINNER, POTATOES AND BUTTERMILK

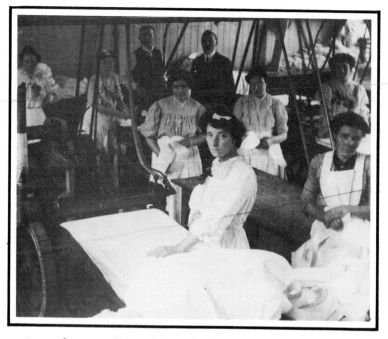

Previous page: To keep the farm intact not all family members could marry and the maiden aunt became another social legacy from the Famine. In return for her labour she received food and shelter.

Left: Derry shirtmakers: a chronic shortage of jobs for men meant that these women were also the family breadwinners.

Below: In the absence of employment opportunities for men in Dublin, the responsibility of providing for the family often fell to women.

Opposite: Selling oddments at a streetmarket meant a crucial extra shilling for the family's budget.

Apart from washing of household articles and clothes, a great deal of scrubbing with soap and water went on continually. The floors, the yard, the step outside the front door, the window sills, the street outside down to the kerb, had all to be attended to, often with the woman of the house on her knees with scrubbing brush and floor cloth.

Anon. 'The Dunmoyle Street Environment 1909–1914'. MS, PRO Belfast.

This devotion to hygiene was probably shared by the wives of Dublin's artisans whose regular comfortable income afforded their families rent for a house owned by the Dublin Artisans' Dwelling Co., and the private sanitation and water supply this entailed. Prior to marriage, those women may well have been employed in one of Dublin's few industries to be staffed by women, Jacob's biscuit factory. Having started work at fourteen, and although earning the low wages common to women of the time, conditions were reasonable and the factory warm, dry and clean. In what must have been almost radically benign

44

Opposite: Women carrying burdens on their heads were a common sight. Babies were carried along in a shawl while older children were often left to fend for themselves.

Below: In districts where roads were few and donkeys expensive it was women who hauled the heavy loads, be it turf from the bog or produce to the fair.

Right: The primitive life in the west added considerably to the women's work load. Corn is ground here as in the Stone Age. The boy on the right is dressed in a petticoat for fear the fairies might carry him off. Girls, being of less value, were safe.

circumstances, the women could avail of a subsidised canteen, resident nurse and free medical and dental services.

Such comfort, care and cleanliness were completely beyond the experience of the women of Dublin's labouring class. Access to water was difficult, and besides, in a tenement room stripped bare by pawning off almost all household articles, there was little left to scrub. Shopping was done daily and food, even staples like tea and sugar were bought in two ounce quantities. To buy in bulk would have created storage problems as there were few cupboards or dressers and besides, a family could not be trusted not to eat a week's rations in a couple of days. When money was low and food scarce, women stood last in line for a meal. The husband, without whose health the family might be destined for the poorhouse, was fed first and best. After him, the children needed to be nourished and only when all were satisfied might the wife eat. Without money, and with

46

scant reason to remain at home, the women of Dublin's tenements were thus forced to work for a more well-to-do family as char- or washer-women, or to sell fruit or fish from a barrow. With the few shillings thus earned the 'slate' in the local grocery could be cleared, perhaps the bed from the pawnshop redeemed or possibly refreshment taken in the local public house. The latter appears to have been popular and drunken women were a not uncommon sight.

For all the squalour, destitution and deprivation of her life it was to the women that Dublin's tenements owed their spirit, camaraderie and sense of kinship for which they became renowned. In the fight for survival, they supported each other by mutual gossip, sharing of child care, and copious loans of anything from a pinch of tea to a 'loan of a pig's foot to grease the cabbage'.

If the women of the tenements played an important role in the life of labouring, the women of the western seaboard played a role which was, if anything, even more crucial and central. With husbands away in Scotland or the richer lands of Tyrone working as migrant labourers, almost the entire responsibility for the production of food, winter warmth, and earnings of cash for the shop fell to the women. Indeed, even if a husband was available there seems to have been no cultural bar to a woman working in the fields, carrying heavy loads when no donkey was available and generally undertaking all manual labour. A contemporary description of women's work in Garumna, Connemara, in the 1890s describes the feats performed by women in just one locality:

The women, besides their ordinary domestic duties, take part in all field work of every description, cut and carry turf and seaweed for manure. In the case of the Lettermullan women they have to carry the turf home in baskets on their backs, a distance of over four miles. They shear the sheep, an operation looked on as women's work and, as a rule only carried out piecemeal, just as much wool being taken as is required and no more. They card, dye and spin the wool thus obtained; they rear fowl for the eggs which are either bartered for goods or sold to the shopkeepers at a rate varying from 10s. the long hundred [120] in winter, to 3s.6d. in summer. They also gather carageen moss from the rocks at low tide which they dry in the sun and sell at from fourpence to sixpence a stone.

The Royal Commission on Congestion in Ireland, 1907.

Egg production was of prime importance to a woman as the money it earned was her only available source of income. Having reared all the other animals of the farm her husband stepped forward at market time, doing all the haggling and dealing – and pocketing the proceeds! Egg money on the other hand was seen as rightfully hers, hence its importance. Unfortunately the shopkeeper, who was also the local egg merchant, often refused to pay cash for eggs – giving tea instead, which her family needed and on which he made a handsome profit.

Left: The work of servants was central to the composure of middle class women.

Above: Spinning wool in County Sligo. The growing girl learns her role in a society where women's work is ceaseless while the man is a bystander.

Opposite: Loving smiles undimmed by poverty.

The need to make cash to help raise her family above subsistence level also forced a woman of the west to undertake craft work such as knitting, lace-making and embroidery. It was an unequal struggle however; a woman working in virtually all her free time would be lucky to earn £5 per annum. In a situation of desperate poverty anything helped.

An old woman in the west, too feeble to continue such a life of strenuous hardship became very dependent on her children for support in widowhood. Small wonder then, that she encouraged her sons to stay at home on the land. For the daughters, however, she envisaged a different future and every assistance and encouragement would be given to the girls to emigrate. It was important to these women to feel they had not reared another generation of females to carry on the unequal struggle while carrying the heaviest burden.

Below left: The matriarch surrounded by her family in 1867. Her husband adopts a distant pose and doubtless an even more distant role from the family.

Below: The woman in this family was the lucky daughter for whom a dowry could be afforded and marriage and family made possible. For her sisters the options were to remain single or to emigrate.

Opposite: Washday. . .The woman probably considered herself lucky to have piped water.

A life of more material comfort attended the woman of the prosperous rural areas of Ireland. Not for her the work of the fields or the beast of burden. At the same time however, her life was much more circumscribed than that of her counterpart in Dublin, the west or Belfast. She was more confined to the house and farmyard than in the past, and, with furnishings, crockery and a comparatively well-dressed family the demand for an increased standard of housekeeping rose. The beginning of the creamery movement in the late nineteenth century meant that traditional areas of her expertise such as butter- and cream-making were no longer open to her, with an attendant loss of status.

Though in more luxurious surroundings, the women of Dublin's wealthier classes led lives which were almost as confined as those of the comfortable rural farmer. Having been driven from central Dublin by high rates and fear of disease, they set up home in the suburbs near congenial neighbours with whom they could share sports and pastimes. A house in Rathgar or Dalkey meant that a husband could travel to the city on business, whilst the woman remained, keeping the cycle of social calls and entertainment moving smoothly. The management of the family's servants also fell to the wife; often three servants had to be administered, a cook, kitchen maid and parlour maid with the addition of a nursery maid if the family contained young children. A servant from the country was preferred by these women, rather than a Dublin girl, as they were seen as healthier, more docile and less likely to have followers! Thus backed by a retinue of able-bodied workers, the new woman of the suburbs was free to call on friends, leave cards or organise an 'At Home' where friends might be entertained by the hostess's social accomplishments, singing or piano playing.

However leisured the lives of women in the middle classes, there can be no doubt that the passing of Victorian life in Ireland would not be mourned by the majority – for indeed, they had little to mourn.

CHAPTER FOUR

The Catholic Church

In the late nineteenth century the Catholic Church, no longer the hidden Church of penal times which maintained a low profile in back streets, emerged assured of its position as the dominant religion.

The new spirit of triumphalism was reflected in the choice of prominent sites for the building of many large high-spired churches. In this major programme of building and adornment the more simple church of penal days was replaced by ornate, often neo-Gothic buildings, boasting elaborate high altars, organs and a variety of statues and devotional ornaments such as the Stations of the Cross. Many of these were added to replace a more 'celtic' practice and to comply with new Roman style liturgies such as Benediction, Forty Hours Adoration and missions.

Such a programme of expansion gave much local employment, both to labourers and stone cutters. However, as bishops and priests tended to favour Italian marble for high altars, and Italian devotional objects generally, much was imported, leading to regular complaints from the then 'Buy Irish' movement. One native firm was able to take advantage of the church building boom, that of James Pearse, father of the 1916 leader Padraic. The cost of these advances was expensive: the interior alone of Armagh cathedral cost £30,000 while Cobh cathedral was completed early in this century for £300,000. Emigrant sons and daughters contributed to the building of the new church at home, as well as local donors, of course.

The resulting Gothic and Italian architecture and artefacts introduced a new art form to Ireland, perhaps the only one accessible to the poor. The new open atmosphere of a church secure in its society gave many an opportunity for a day of fun and festivity in an otherwise restricted social life. In particular, First Communion day was appreciated by children as one of their few occasions of celebration, marked by special clothes. On this day, women, too, enjoyed one of the rare outings available to a section of the community otherwise tied to the home or field.

Traditionally, religious practices in rural Ireland had integrated into a life heavily governed by the agricultural season. Old pagan festivals had also been assimilated; hence, for example, the custom of climbing Croagh Patrick on the last Sunday of July, the old pagan festival of Lughnasa and bonfire night being held on St John's Eve. Holy wells held a respected place in this traditional religion, and many were associated with different saints and

with different dates. Pilgrimages to holy wells combined both religion and festivity; people visited the wells in groups for praying, eating and drinking. Each well had its own religious ritual attached, and various sites were said to cure different ailments. The newly emerging Catholic Church, however, increasingly frowned on such practices, regarding them as a hangover from a superstitious past. The holy wells, therefore, gradually became deserted and fell into disuse. Similarly, patterns and wakes disappeared in the new 'devotional revolution' and more formal observances

Page 53: Loyalty to the Church and religious devotion transcended all barriers of class and an entire town would turn out for the Corpus Christi procession.

Above: The Penal Church remembered.

Right: The High Altar, Monaghan Cathedral. . .One of the few art forms available to all came with the more 'Roman' churches built in Ireland in the nineteenth century.

Opposite: The large building drive undertaken by the Church provided work and badly needed cash for labourers in poorer communities.

such as retreats, Benediction and processions took their place.

The priests in the vanguard of this 'revolution' came overwhelmingly from the families of large farmers and shopkeepers. There was no shortage of vocations and while the population of Ireland halved, the number of priests doubled. Religious observance was strong in the people of Ireland, and unlike many other countries, religion was practised faithfully regardless of class; even the most destitute were regular church attenders. Religion acted as a social bond linking both middle and working classes. In fact, it was frequently the priest who was the only member of the middle class to penetrate the lives of the poor.

Given the background of the majority of the priests, it was natural that the Church began to reflect the values of the section of society from which they came. They sympathised fully with the Land War and with demands for Home Rule. From their farming and rural backgrounds priests also understood the newly felt need for the farm to be passed on intact to one son, realising as they did the dangers of subdivision of land. Also, they fully sympathised with the farmers' emphasis on matchmaking and dowries as vital instruments to ensure the heir to the farm would marry only when the father declared the time was right – and that he would marry the right woman. It was important, therefore, that undue social contact between young people should be prevented and so, the characteristic image of the priest with the blackthorn stick emerges: preventing crossroad dances and preaching against the sins of the flesh. The co-operation between Church and family pressure prevailed; before the Famine the average age for women to marry was twenty-four to twenty-five and twenty-eight to twenty-nine for men. By the eve of the First World War, this had soared to thirty for women and thirty-five for men. One in four women never married at all and many, finding the regime restrictive, emigrated.

Other temporal concerns of the people induced the Church to action. The Society of St Vincent de Paul

Below: Piety, St Columb's Wells, Derry.

Opposite: The Celtic Church survived longest in the west of Ireland where Christianity and paganism fused. On the right are crutches and bandages left behind by those cured at this Holy Well.

DOON WELL.KILMACRENAN. Co.DONEGAL .9330.W.L.

recognised drunkenness as the source of many problems of poverty in cities, and groups such as the Dublin Total Abstinence Society ran regular temperance meetings. Clergy of all denominations united in denouncing the evils of drink and in administering total abstinence pledges. These, allied with temperance bands and marches, were highly effective and a growing level of sobriety soon became apparent. Nor was the Church unaware of the poverty which surrounded it at the time. Pope Leo XII in his Encyclical of May 1891, 'The Condition of the Working Classes', declared:

Neither must it be supposed that the solicitude of the Church is so preoccupied with the spiritual concerns of her children as to neglect their temporal and earthly interests. Her desire is that the poor, for example, should rise above poverty and wretchedness, and better their condition in life, and for this she makes a strong

Opposite: The demise of the Celtic Church and the development of the newer Roman liturgy brought liturgical rites such as Benediction and processions. As one of the few legitimate reasons to escape from hearth and home, religious festivities were greatly welcomed by women.

Right, top: The landlord and the parish priest would have little difficulty finding common ground for conversation. . .Both were leaders in the local community, and the priest, coming from a farming family himself, understood the concerns of the landed gentry.

Right, bottom: Although the creamery movement was founded and fostered by Horace Plunkett, at local level success depended on the organisational skills of the clergy.

endeavour. By the very fact that she calls men to virtue and forms them to its practice she promotes this in no small degree.

A parish priest in Dublin reported that:

... a few years ago I wrote very strongly from my twenty-one years' experience in the Pro-Cathedral Parish, but all our pleading perished before the slum-owners' widespread influence and interest. I recall with clinging realism my countless visits, at all hours of the night, to the pestilent slum-rooms, in each of which five or six poor creatures, and often more, would be found inhaling, through their sleep, the night through, the foul and fetid air that worsened hour by hour. It is only one who comes from out of the fresh air of the midnight streets into the crowded slum-room that at all realizes the intolerable and prostrating smells in which the poor must take their unrefreshing slumbers.

John Robert O'Connell. The Problem of the Dublin Slums. *Hodges Figgis, Dublin, 1913.*

Many Catholic charities of the time showed to the poor the practical face of Christian caring. It must be admitted at the same time that one of their motivations was a fear that Catholic children would be attracted to various Protestant sects by free clothing, outings and other inducements. Organisations such as the Society of St Vincent de Paul, while being hampered by the fact that its potential members and benefactors no longer lived in the city and had moved almost beyond reach to the suburbs, still maintained a proud record of vital aid to those in need. Many Dublin families indeed owed their survival to them.

Thus the dark days had ended for the Church. Large new buildings testified to the status which it had now achieved and the Church began to play an increasingly strong role in the social and political life of the country. The Catholic Church had entered a new era.

Opposite: An important role for clergy in the west was to accompany officials of the Congested Districts Board on their inspections. They lobbied for a share of the development work of the board to be established in their parishes.

Right: Religious orders provided the only care available for the handicapped, the orphaned and sick in the days before the welfare state.

CHAPTER FIVE

The Dublin Slums

The nineteenth century was to be decisive in Dublin's history. In the early 1800s, the city was at the height of its splendour, the home of nobility, and graced by fine buildings and parks. By tragic contrast, at the close of that same century, the capital was in ruins, pitted by derelict sites, its nobility vanished and the remaining population demoralised by unemployment and almost vanquished by poverty.

Such devastation was brought about by greed and immorality, official incompetence and neglect. The first death knell sounded when Grattan's Parliament was dissolved and the Act of Union took place in 1801. No longer would Dublin be the seat of Parliament and the centre of its own universe – it would soon become a neglected backwater. 'Society' moved to London and took with it the wealth which would otherwise have been invested in indigenous industry. Dublin would therefore escape the worst excesses of England's industrial revolution, but the price was enormous.

Without native wealth, industries in Dublin faltered and then died until the only significant ones remaining were brewing, distilling and biscuit-making. Apart from these stalwarts, only unskilled and labouring work was available in the city, much of it in the docks into which were imported almost all the manufactured goods required by the country and from which agricultural produce mainly was exported. For these low-skilled jobs wages were pitifully small, the average being eighteen shillings per week. Class differences in the city were enormous – a Grafton Street shop at the same time was advertising ladies' summer suits at over eight times those eighteen shillings.

Meanwhile, Dublin was declining against the background of an ailing agricultural sector, with the result that people from country areas began to crowd into the city in search of work. These new migrants were to thrive in their new home. Healthier and sturdier than their wretched city counterparts, they successfully applied for jobs in the police force and in companies such as Guinness's. Similarly, an unseen network of people from 'back home' already established in the city, ensured their entry to trades and the better lifestyle this could buy. Because of their regular income, they could afford higher rents than the unskilled Dubliners, and so could aspire to being housed by Dublin

Corporation or the Artisans' Dwelling Company – the hallmark of the working class. Between 1821 and 1891 the population of Dublin grew by 66,400. When we remember that the city area referred to is that bounded by the two canals, an area of 3807 acres, we have some understanding of the congestion in Dublin: 65.6 people per acre.

One of the first requirements of a growing population is, of course, shelter, and it was here, after the lack of employment opportunities, that Dublin most betrayed her citizens. Tenement houses, as they were called, once the grand Georgian dwellings of the now departed wealthy, became home to Dublin's poor. But whereas a house once had sheltered one family, now they were subdivided and often sheltered as many as five or six families.

Tenements	occupied by	Families
3270		1–5
1778		6–10
104		11–15
8		16–19
1		24

In summary, Dublin housed almost 26,000 families in tenement houses and 7800 of those in one-roomed lettings.

Such overcrowded conditions had not gone unnoticed and there was no shortage of inquiries into health and living conditions in the tenements. Acts of Parliament to improve the situation abounded, and were passed in 1866, 1867, 1868, 1875, 1879, 1882, 1890 and again in 1908. We can

Page 63: Casual work on the docks was one of the few jobs open to the men of Dublin's tenements. Work was plentiful during spring and autumn, peak times for cattle exports.

Opposite: The residents of one Dublin tenement on their doorstep. In the early 1800s one Dublin family and its servants lived there. The flight of the middle classes to the new suburbs made houses available which were sub-divided to accommodate the growing population of the unskilled.

Right: Two shoeshiners at work on Capel Street Bridge. Poor education and a lack of skills and influential contacts meant a life of badly paid and unskilled work.

Below: The room which housed a Dublin family. Sickness and unemployment meant that most of their goods would be pawned, leaving only bare necessities.

only surmise now that two essential ingredients necessary for their implementation were absent – money and political will. The lack of the latter may have been caused by the fact that when the nobility and gentry departed from Dublin, they were soon followed by the city's new middle classes who left for emerging suburbs such as Dalkey, Rathmines and Pembroke. Although their businesses were situated in the city, they now paid rates to their new boroughs. Those remaining were elected to Dublin Corporation and their record in improving the city is less than praiseworthy. Indeed, some of the members of the Corporation, Alderman O'Reilly, Corrigan and Crozier, were owners of tenements. Such owners were entitled to tax rebates on rent from tenements if they carried out improvements to their property. It was not unusual, however, for some landlords to obtain waivers from these improvements and still be in receipt of the tax rebate, as happened with Aldermen O'Reilly and Corrigan, who obtained their waivers from Sir Charles Cameron, the then Medical Officer of Health.

Opposite: One family to a room, all the residents of this courtyard shared a single water tap. The cross painted on the left denotes the house was unfit for human habitation – due for demolition. However, such houses sheltered families for many more years.

Right: Owning no property and therefore disenfranchised, the poor of Dublin could afford to ignore the election poster. The real business of the day was to rummage through stalls for second-hand clothing.

Below: This family was lucky to own a bed and table. A box by the fireside served as a chair. The food on the table and utensils on the floor highlight the lack of storage facilities. Clothes by the fire show the laundering difficulties faced.

The inevitable happened in September 1913 in Church Street when two tenements collapsed. Had all forty people who lived there been at home it would have been a major tragedy, but, nevertheless, seven were killed. Considering the age of the tenements and the fact that their walls were filled with timber which had rotted, bulged and weakened the walls, it is amazing that more such tragedies did not occur. The response to the deaths in Church Street was swift, and a public sworn inquiry was appointed by the Local Government Board for Ireland to 'inquire into the Housing Conditions of the Working Classes in the City of Dublin'.

The committee reported in 1914, and having heard from seventy-six witnesses and visited the tenements, their outrage at their discoveries can be seen breaking through their parliamentary and measured language. Among the

first of the ills of the tenements to be listed was invariably the dirt. The hall and stairways used in common by perhaps six families were described as 'exceedingly foul', and the filth of the backyard and front area so polluted as to 'beggar description'. The committee found human excrement scattered about the yards of the tenements in nearly every tenement visited and in many cases even in the passages of the houses. The toilets, shared as they were by thirty or more people, were putrid. All water for cooking, cleaning and washing had to be carried in buckets, often up eight flights of stairs.

Cleanliness, then, for individual families demanded almost superhuman effort. The committee found it gratifying to report that in many instances efforts had been made by families to keep their rooms tidy and clean. Furniture for these rooms was scarce and might consist only of tables and chairs; in bad times – during sickness or unemployment – these were quickly dispensed with and replaced by boxes. The one or two beds in which all the family slept would also be sold or pawned and in their place would appear a 'repellent assortment of rags' as the family's resting place. Ovens and stoves were almost unknown in

Opposite: Country people return home to Lucan after a visit to the capital. Seats on top, although exposed to the elements, were cheaper.

Right: Grafton Street, Dublin, c.1905. Automobiles had arrived, costing up to £1,000 each. Prices were to fall dramatically with the introduction of Mr Ford's Model T to Ireland in 1910.

Dublin's tenements and all cooking was done on the open fire. But, in fact, little cooking was done anyway as the meagre budget often bought only bread and tea for two of the day's meals. Even in worst times efforts would be made to provide a good dinner for the family breadwinner, as without his health and strength life would be even worse. Vegetables other than potatoes, cabbage and onions were rarely cooked and to these might be added cheap American bacon or herrings to complete the dinner. Fruit, desserts, cakes and sweets were almost never seen and the diet was wearying in its monotony.

Poor diet combined with squalid living conditions were a recipe for a variety of ailments which were to plague Dublin's poor. Tuberculosis was to the forefront of these and decimated families for almost another generation before being finally eradicated. Forty years previously, the physician-in-charge at Cork Street Fever Hospital had attempted to show the connection between bad sanitation and a high incidence of fever – typhus, enteritis, etc. These houses he termed 'fever nests' and described a typical one, in Bridgefoot Street, as follows:

This house is entered from the street by a passage, with a black and rotten floor, in which are open chinks communicating with the cellar below; the boards are damp, and sodden with dirt;

Opposite: Union Jacks above the St Stephen's Green Club. Electric trams appeared in Dublin in 1896 and were mainly used by the suburban commuters as, unlike English industrial cities, their hours and routes followed did not suit the labourers of the city.

Below: A Dublin playground provides light musical relief for the families of the crumbling tenements in the background.

going upwards we find things somewhat better, but the whole upper part of the house is dilapidated; going downwards, we first come to the entrance of a small back yard, a place covered ankle-deep with human filth, a privy and ash-pit totally unapproachable without passing through a sea of dirt, a water-tap running, and washing such of the dirt as is within reach into a pipe sewer which runs through the cellar of the house, and which had a hole through which the sewage passed into the cellar, converting it into a cesspool; this cellar was immediately beneath two rooms inhabited by a family of fifteen, every one of whom has enteric fever. In the same street I find another house with all these characteristics repeated, except the broken sewer, but this house had no sewer at all.

Thomas W. Grimshaw M.D. Remarks on the Prevalence and Distribution of Fever in Dublin. Fannin & Co., Dublin, 1872.

Typhus had still not been eradicated by the early twentieth century and caused thirteen deaths in the years 1902 to 1911. Its place as a major killer disease had been overtaken however by tuberculosis, which in the same period killed 1444 of Dublin's citizens. Other diseases of poverty and overcrowding, such as pneumonia and enteritis, claimed 4600 lives. By contrast rickets, scabies and lice, although a scourge in themselves, were mere inconveniences.

A brief oblivion from squalour, monotony and hardship was devoutly sought and few resisted the lures of the local public house where for the price of a bottle of stout you would also get heat, light, comfort and companionship. And if too much money was spent there, the one and only suit could be pawned on Monday morning and redeemed again the following Saturday in time for Sunday Mass.

When the departmental committee finally reported to Parliament, they recommended the acquisition of derelict sites and the building of new houses for the working classes. Feeling that this ought to be the responsibility of Dublin Corporation, the committee rejected the suggestion that a separate housing authority be established. In a separate rider to the report one of the committee's members, J.F.

Above: Peamount Sanatorium, founded by Lady Aberdeen and the Women's Health Association to care for the victims of tuberculosis from the tenements. The sanatorium had its own herd of cattle to provide TB-free milk.

Opposite: Farmers from neighbouring counties arrived at Smithfield at 4.00 a.m. on hay market days, Tuesdays and Fridays. Spreading hay under their carts they slept there until the day's business began. Customers were hay retailers from nearby Bow Street and Stirrup Lane who sold it to local businesses for their horses.

McCabe, insisted that no piecemeal building programme be undertaken until an entire plan for the city's development was drafted. He was convinced that 'To build without a Town Plan in the old City will prevent effectually Dublin ever becoming what it should be – as beautiful as it own surroundings.'

Meanwhile, Dublin's downtrodden waited, unemployed, ailing and poor in a huddled, and far from beautiful city.

CHAPTER SIX

Fashion

If it is true that by the clothes we wear we make many statements about ourselves, our lifestyle and values, the wealthy of the Victorian era imparted many messages through their wardrobes. Most importantly, by the use of high quality material and many adornments they announced to the onlooker that they were, indeed, very wealthy. Although the men had cast aside the ornate silks and wigs of earlier centuries, their sober black suits showed they were industrious people, office- or bank-bound, while their white collars and cuffs indicated that they would remain clean – they did not have to get dirty to earn a living. More casual clothing was worn by men only for sports such as golf or shooting.

Although men by this time had to dress in a practical manner, women of the middle and upper classes were still creatures of leisure and their clothes reflected this. Nothing much by way of activity could be expected of the wearer of a crinoline, and an observer would also be aware that servants were available to wash, press and mend such an elaborate garment. Many dresses contained dozens of tiny hooks and buttons which could not be closed without the help of a maid, and the ladies' elaborate hairstyles also called for much time and assistance.

Although frowned upon by Queen Victoria and by her coroners who denounced them as a fire risk, the crinoline dominated the fashion world from the 1850s to the 1870s.

So awkward a garment was it that when ladies went shopping they were unable to leave their carriages and the goods had to be brought out to them for inspection instead.

The need for practicality was still not uppermost when the bustle replaced the crinoline in 1870. Considered ultrafeminine and seductive, these dresses were extremely tight and allowed little room for walking. *The Ladies' Treasury* wrote in 1876 that 'skirts are now so tight that our sitting and walking are seriously inconvenienced, the smallest steps in walking are indispensable and it is impossible to sit any way, but on one's side.'

The waists of the ladies who wore these garments were as tiny as corsets and the wearer's sense of martyrdom could make them. From an early age, Victorian girls were heavily laced into corsets, the laces being pulled tighter and tighter by the maid while the unfortunate victim pulled against the bedpost. The resulting waist measurements of sixteen, seventeen or eighteen inches were greatly admired. One ladies' tailor wrote in 1897: 'It is quite clear that comfort is not essential with women, but the fit is everything. You cannot pay a woman a greater compliment than to make her so tight in the waist that she is miserable.'

She was more than miserable, in fact. Doctors increasingly denounced tight lacing as causing damage to reproductive organs and being responsible for many complications in childbirth. Sense was to prevail ultimately

and the bustle and accompanying punishing lacing had disappeared by the mid 1890s. Skirts became simpler, so simple that many complained that they looked like dressing gowns from behind. To compensate, sleeves became elaborate leg-of-mutton type, with ornamental stitching and finishing.

The craze for cycling in the 1890s and later the arrival of the motor car did much to liberate fashion, and its wearers, both men and women. Blouses became highly fashionable and were worn either with skirts or, for the very daring, knickerbockers – one male tailor feared the impact on a lady's modesty of having to have her knees measured! Men's cycling costumes were enlivened by straw boaters, knickerbockers or breeches. At this stage the motor car was still open to the elements and a large range of loose coats, waterproofs and scarves to protect hairstyles appeared on the fashion scene.

Gradually, fashion also began to reflect the arrival of the 'new woman' who was interested in the suffragette move-

Page 75: Crinolined ladies of early Victorian times. The layered crinoline on the right is trimmed with silk/wool Paisley fabric of the time (1855-60). The hats, for garden use only, are Leghorn straw with lace veil attached.

Opposite: Promenade at the races. Gentleman on left wears more old fashioned 'Ascot' morning suit, while his more fashionable companion on the right wears a more modern (1905-09) double breasted suit with narrow tie. The ladies' parasols and the nets worn over their faces protect them from sunshine, dust and grime.

Right, above: Alexandra, Princess of Wales, the fashion trendsetter of her time. Her high collars and 'dog-collars' of pearls, which dominated the fashion of the time, originated in her desire to conceal a scar on her neck.

Right, below: Family in mourning, following the fashion for mourning set by Queen Victoria. The mother's hair ornament of seed pearls was very popular (*c.* 1890). The emphasis on naval power is reflected in the girls' sailor-style clothes. The baby's sash is tied on the left to show that it is a boy.

Left: Tennis party. Gentleman in left foreground wears sports shoes, although not yet of canvas, as was later fashionable. Most men in the group wear white flannels; and the women's tight-fitting sleeves must have been most unsuitable for the game.

Insert, above: Connemara homespun.

Opposite: Working women stand beside the carriage, the nurse in outdoor uniform; the woman helping the man down the steps shows by her uniform-style dress and fob watch that she, too, is a staff member (1880s).

ment, and even in going out to work. Clothes became simpler and more comfortable and skirts rose ever so slightly so that ankles were visible. Day clothes could now be open at the neck, and hats, which had been gigantic, became small toques with perhaps a feather for adornment. The Victorian age, when both furniture and fashion were dark and heavily upholstered, had finally passed.

'Fashionable' is not, of course, a term which can truthfully be applied to the clothing worn by the majority of the population in the mid to late nineteenth century.

Apart from the wealthy, all that was required of clothing was that it be cheap and that the wearer be modest and protected from the elements. Style, elegance and fashion were considerations for others.

Traditionally, the people of the west of Ireland were almost self-sufficient in clothing: the wool, having been sheared from the family's own sheep, was carded and spun and then dyed using local mosses and lichens. The yarn was then sent to a local weaver and the resulting cloth was made up into the family's clothes. Sometimes this was done by an

itinerant tailor who came and lived temporarily with the family while making their clothes. With improvement in communications and when new roads opened up the west, travelling stalls came to fairs and markets and readymade clothes were gradually introduced. Family members returning from work in England or Scotland often wore shop-bought clothes which were the envy of all who wore the rough-sewn garments traditional in the west. By the end of the century the new look had triumphed and shop clothes were definitely preferred and worn – for example, hats instead of shawls – by those who had the cash to buy them.

The clothes worn by the poor of the cities had already served a

Opposite: The fashionable young man wears a shorter morning coat, spats and silver grey tie. Both other men display the styles from which his outfit has sprung: on the left the slightly longer jacket with cut-away tails, on the right full morning wear. The women's skirts are descendants of the hobble, but with pleating to allow ease of movement (*c.* 1910-12).

Above: Somewhat unusually, these bathers do not wear the white canvas swimming shoes common at the time. The woman second from the right is the most fashionable: her suit is sleeveless, the legs tighter, the cumberbund wider. The bathing caps are of rubber and the suits are of black or navy woollen stockinet, which stretched when wet! (1900s).

Right: Irish Lace Industries Depot, Grafton Street, Dublin. Lace borders could be bought here by the yard and brought to a dressmaker. The guards and sticks of the fans were imported from Paris, the lace supplied by the women of the west of Ireland.

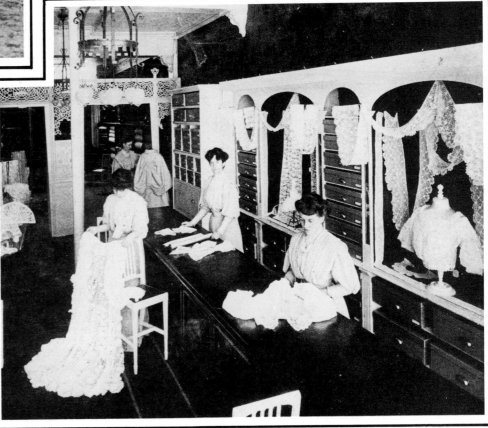

Opposite: The new woman and the old. The latter wears a hat of 1880-90s. Her cloak is traditional. Note also the metal clip which lifts the front of her skirt, not only to make walking easier but also to save the front hem from dirt and wear. The woman on the left is, at least comparatively, dressed for easier movement. Her chatelaine, which hangs from her waist into her pocket, carries her keys, watch and pencil.

Above: Family croquet: The mother announces her more casual approach by being unadorned by jewellery and by wearing no gloves – highly unusual for ladies. Her tightly bodiced jacket extends down the front to the curves of the 'apron' which is then drawn up at the back to form a bustle. Similarly, her daughter's apron is merely decorative. Note the untidy schoolboy look and bulging pockets of the son!

long and useful life, especially those worn by children. In an age when clothing was not seen as disposable and was expected to last if not a lifetime then certainly for many years, a garment had usually given its original owner much service before being passed down the social ladder. A dress made with tight sleeves and a bustle in the 1880s would have had its bustle removed and the sleeves let out in the 1890s; it might have been dyed several times to give it a new lease of life and its waistline would have been adjusted to accommodate the growing matronly figure of my lady. Only then, when its use had been finally exhausted, would

Left: The arrival of a new invention – the safety pins which hold the woman's blouse on the right. They would probably have been bought at the fair, as would the skirt worn by the woman on the left, a cast-off from townsfolk. The toothless smile of the woman on the left is a legacy from the sugar used to sweeten the Indian meal which supplemented the diet in the west.

Opposite, left: Self-sufficiency of the west reflected in homespun clothes; the buttons, including those of the lapels, are Irish-made, of horn, and the crios is used as a belt.

Opposite, right: Shoe translators at work, repairing shoes for Dublin's second-hand markets. The woman in background wears a late nineteenth century hat, and her cloak is a blanket fastened at the neck with a pin.

it find its way to the second-hand stalls such as those in Dublin's Daisy Market. A woman of the tenements would then become its owner for a few pence, and by combining it with a shawl would thus be clothed for a year. Her shoes came from a similar stall, as did those for most of the city's adult poor. Old shoes were specially imported from England in large quantities, and then mended by the 'shoe translators' who sold them. By the time a garment had reached its final owner – a child of the tenements for whom it had been simply hacked down to size – it was indeed a ragged and exhausted object.

CHAPTER SEVEN

Children

I thank the goodness and the grace
Which on my birth have smiled,
And made me, in these Christian days,
A happy English child.
Recited by children in a west of Ireland school.

The idea of childhood as a time of leisure, fun and innocence, free from adult duties and economic concerns, was a concept experienced by only very few in Victorian Ireland. Whether the child's parents lived in a Dublin tenement, a Belfast 'two-up, one-down', or on a farm in the west of Ireland, a cruel reality was brought to bear soon after infancy.

In Belfast, reality loomed large when, at the age of eight, many children went to work as 'halftimers' in the linen mills. The education authorities did not allow children to work fulltime until they were twelve, but at eight they could work three days a week and attend school, which was run by the mill owners, on two and a half days. Belfast's children did not endure the abject poverty and deprivation of their country cousins in the west of Ireland or of those in the Dublin slums, but they paid a high price for the greater financial ease of their lives.

Robert Lynd, in his book *Home Life in Ireland* (published London 1904), reports

The deadliest sin in the labour conditions of Ireland . . . is the system under which boys and girls hardly out of their infancy are employed in the mills at a wage of 3s. 6d. a week.

In Ulster the child works full time during three days in the week, and attends school on the remaining days. The results which follow, when children of twelve years old or thereabouts are kept working for ten hours a day during three days in the week in a humid atmosphere of from 70 to 80 degrees Fahrenheit, might have been foreseen. Vitality is slowly squeezed out of them, and it is hardly an exaggeration to say that

from the age of 15 upwards they die like flies.

The death rate in Belfast among young people between the ages of 15 and 20 is double what it is in Manchester . . . there can be little doubt that the half-time system is a ruling cause of such an unnatural rate of mortality.

Not only were conditions in the factories humid and hot, but the machinery emitted an overwhelming and ceaseless noise. The children working in such an environment dared not suffer a lapse of either concentration or co-ordination, for to do so meant perhaps an arm being caught in a carding machine. Subsequent amputation would mean permanent disability and, with no compensation payable, certain destitution.

Some simple pleasures helped lighten an otherwise tough

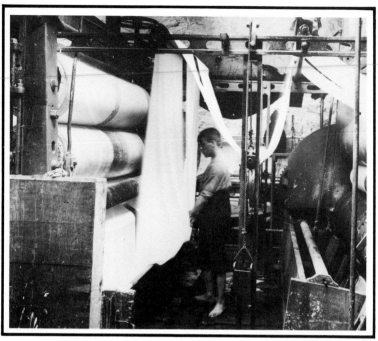

Previous page: Child worker at Bridewell, Chancery Street, Dublin.

Left: Dublin docks, a favourite mitching venue. John Cooke, treasurer of N.S.P.C.C., reported: 'In no city in these islands with which I am acquainted have the children such a freedom, I might say such possession of the streets as Dublin. Many thousands of little ones throng the thoroughfares, under no control, running moral and physical risks. Ill-clad, ill-fed, ill-disciplined . . . Numbers never rise out of slum life.'

Above: Fulltime workers were recruited in the linen mills at thirteen years of age. After learning the techniques from experienced workers for six to eight weeks, during which they received no pay, they were given a machine of their own.

Opposite: Glorious mud pies at Dolphin's Barn, Dublin. The horse dung with which the mud was mixed helped spread disease to children whose resistance to infection was already impaired by inadequate diet. If they did succumb, £1 was required to bury a small child in Glasnevin – more than a labourer's weekly wage. With coffin and hearse costing even more, and the horror of a pauper burial almost an obsession, almost all the poor paid burial insurance which they could ill afford.

existence. Little children might receive a halfpenny a week as pocket money on father's pay day, Saturday. Parents would have six holidays a year: two days at Christmas, two at Easter and two in July. With a sense of great adventure the family would board a horse-tram to Glengormley, there to enjoy the hobby horses, swings and a day of fun and frolic.

Small as it was, such a day's enjoyment was totally foreign to the experience of the children of the smallholdings in the west of Ireland. Enlisted in the family's struggle to wrench a living where none was possible, childhood ended soon after infancy. It was an infancy which may well have been indulged by the grandmother, but it came to an abrupt end when, as soon as they were capable, children were expected to become the farm labourers which their families could not, of course, afford to hire. In the fields they turned and then picked the potatoes, when they were not blighted, that is. On the bogs they stacked turf and hauled it home on their backs, and their visits to the beach were not for pleasure but to pick the seaweed, so essential to the family finances when it was sold for iodine production.

School was but an interruption in the real world of work. When the children of the west did attend, they each carried

Left: The children's charity, Dr. Barnardo's, had pleaded for 'room, room for a child to grow', and Lady Aberdeen responded by establishing playgrounds in Dublin's inner city. The boys here are attending a boxing class in her playground near Ormond Quay, Dublin.

Opposite: Annagry national school. Attendance was not compulsory outside the larger towns until the 1920s. Very young children found the journey to school too onerous, and older children were required to help at home, so school began for many at seven years and finished at twelve, if not before.

a sod of turf to warm the schoolroom. But so seldom did they attend, being needed at home on the farm to herd cattle among other jobs, that an inspector of schools remarked that one factor alone would increase school attendance tenfold – proper fencing in rural Ireland.

Unlike the children of the city tenements, however, one advantage the children of the farms had was that their health was usually good. Used to a hard, robust, outdoor existence, and living on a diet of buttermilk and potatoes, they did not fall victim to the diseases of poverty and overcrowding rampant in cities. Their physique was to stand them in good stead later when they moved to cities in Ireland, to Britain to build roads, further afield to the United States and railway building, or to Australia's goldfields. More immediately, however, it made them marketable commodities at hiring fairs when their families would be paid £2 by a wealthy inland farmer, and the child would become his for half a year. What became of them during that time depended solely on the disposition of the individual farmer; some were treated harshly, the more lucky became almost members of a new family. At first, though, standing barefoot at the hiring fair, being sized up by the farmer as he would a cow, these boys and girls must surely have known shame, humiliation and not a little fear.

Sharing the need for work, but not the opportunity, Dublin's tenement children availed of more haphazard means to add to the family budget. Schools were overcrowded, often with neither toilets nor playgrounds. It must have seemed no hardship, then, to be kept at home as they often were to beg on the streets or to sell newspapers or flowers. Also, since their mothers were often employed as charwomen or selling fruit from a barrow, the children frequently had to stay at home to look after younger family members.

When they did go to school they went barefoot, and often with empty stomachs or having eaten only a meagre breakfast of bread and tea. Few efforts were made to provide slum children with school meals and it was not

Left: Entrance to the Bridewell, Chancery Street, Dublin. The struggle for survival meant that the labour of children was essential.

Opposite: Men ranked highest in the family hierarchy of the west, and this order was reflected in the children. Here, while both are heavily laden, it is the boy who wears the boots.

until 1916 that schools, especially convents, provided breakfast, and some even a midday meal. Such food was vital for children reared on not a lot more than tea, bread and margarine. What milk was available was usually the carrier of tuberculosis; many families preferred canned and highly sweetened condensed milk which, although clean, was nutritionally deficient. Not surprisingly on such a diet, and living in grossly overcrowded and insanitary conditions, the children of the capital suffered appallingly bad health. Many did not survive the first year of life. In 1905, children of labourers, hawkers and porters were fourteen times more likely to die between the ages of one and five than their rich middle class counterparts. The cause of death was often normal childhood illnesses; in 1899, six hundred Dublin children died from measles. Dysentery was prevalent during summer months – hordes of flies thrived on the rubbish tips which littered tenement yards.

A plethora of charities existed to help these slum children. Clothing, boots, picnics and seaside trips were organised by organisations such as the Society of St. Vincent de Paul and the Sick and Indigent Roomkeepers' Society. The Women's National Health Association, under the direction of Ishbel, Countess of Aberdeen, supplied sterilised milk in clean containers to as many mothers as possible.

But such charities merely tinkered with the symptoms of poverty; many of Dublin's children were born in poverty and would live their lives in poverty, as their parents before them. Access to education was difficult as local schools had classes catering only for those under twelve. Apprenticeships were jealously guarded by the artisan class, and the ill-fed puny youths of Dublin usually failed the medical test necessary to work in Guinness's – the pinnacle of achievement for Dublin's working class.

Ill fed and clad as they were, Dublin children, however neglected, seldom suffered cruelty at the hands of their parents. A report of the National Society for the Prevention of Cruelty to Children stated that they needed to 'rarely touch' the parents of the destitute in Dublin. 'They, sharing their misery and destitution with their children, can hardly be said to be cruel.'

A more orderly and regimented life was enjoyed by the children of the middle classes in the fresh sea air of suburbs such as Killiney and Dalkey. The railway line provided

access for their families to the pleasures of Kingstown (Dún Laoghaire) and Bray, where a sedate walk on the pier could be enjoyed or where the bands played to entertain the gentle folk.

Left: Children at harvest time on their family estate in 1904.

Above: A Belfast technical school. Only tradesmen could afford to send their sons here, thus passing on the advantages of a more comfortable life.

Opposite: In a report on living conditions in the Dublin slums a commentator remarked: 'The children go hatless and barefoot, and are frequently dressed in the worn-out clothes of their parents, rudely cut down to fit.'

In schooling, the paths of the boys and girls diverged. Not until the twentieth century had well begun did education become a serious option for girls of the middle classes. Before that music, embroidery and the social graces, taught by an indifferent standard of governesses, was more important for aspiring wives than the classics. Depending on the family's income a young boy of the middle class would be sent to a private college such as Blackrock or Clongowes, or, if in reduced circumstances, to avail of the free secondary schools of the Christian Brothers. Here, the boys would follow a curriculum akin to that taught in the public schools of England. Alternatively, they were enrolled in 'cramming academies' where bright boys were prepared for entrance examinations to the Home or Indian Civil Service. Although for many positions an examination was necessary, there can be no doubt that family connections and influence stood these boys in good stead. Before sitting the examination to work in the banks, for example, it was first necessary to have been nominated by either a governor of the bank or one of its managers. Only then, and having been assessed as 'suitable' at an interview, was a boy allowed to undertake the examination in English and arithmetic. Similarly, clerkship vacancies in the Great Southern and Western Railways were filled only by nomination from the Railways' directors. It was only in 1903 that open competitive examinations were held in the Railways, after public protest at the exclusive nature of the old system.

Nonetheless, the children of Ireland's middle class grew up in a stable, secure world and in the certain knowledge that their futures were to be as safe as their childhood. At the turn of the century, Blackrock College had eighty-nine recent past pupils in religious, legal and medical professions, twenty were college professors, while others held high-ranking positions in the Indian Civil Service and in consular service in China, Japan, Constantinople and Australia.

CHAPTER EIGHT

Sport

Sport, as we know it, is surprisingly, a modern invention, being a legacy from the mid-Victorian era. Prior to then sport was certainly played, but on a local *ad hoc* basis, with rules, scoring systems, and leagues being almost unknown. The popularising of sport and its codification occurred on a worldwide basis, Ireland being no exception to the sweeping phenomenon.

Sporting development in England was a primary influence on its counterpart in Ireland. The healthy development of boys at English public schools was the subject of much discussion among educators who saw as their duty the development of 'muscular christians'. Holiness was no longer to be associated with learning, and manliness was to become as important as classical learning. To be manly was one of the highest aspirations, but it must be remembered that childishness was seen as no bar to manliness; to be effeminate however was the gravest sin. The novel *Tom Brown's Schooldays*, published in 1869, extolling the virtues of muscular christianity, became a huge success and attracted a large cult following. Charles Kingsley, one of the proponents of the new education theory, was principal of Wellington School which was described as fostering: 'The great importance and value of animal spirits, physical strength and hearty enjoyment of all the pursuits and accomplishments which are connected with them.'

Parents whose own sporting activities were of the hunting, shooting, fishing variety, began to be convinced of the character-forming possibilities of games for their sons, and all schools throughout England began to change their emphasis. No longer would it be acceptable to loll around or to walk and talk with one's friends; vigorous and organised physical activity was all. That there were nationalistic and militaristic overtones to the new movement there can be no doubt. The bogey of Napoleon III and the desire to further the empire found a willing response in the public schools, whose regimentation of games was easily transmuted to drilling in the schools' newly established Rifle and Volunteer Corps.

When sixteen-year-old William Ellis ran with the ball instead of claiming a mark at Rugby School, his discovery of the game of rugby may well have been accidental. It was no accident however that its birthplace in Ireland was at

Dublin University, in Trinity College. For years the Irish landed gentry had sent their sons to be educated at public schools in England. While many remained there for university education, many more returned here to Trinity College. Those who arrived back in the mid to late 1800s brought with them the new craze of England's public schools, rugby. Robert Scott who was the Dublin University Rugby Club's first officer in 1855 had been at school in Rugby. Initially, matches were played among inter-Trinity teams there being no opponents outside the college until 1860. Another past pupil of Rugby, Charles Barrington, elected captain in 1867, was to influence greatly the spread of the game in Ireland. Reflecting the codification of the game which was occurring in England, Barrington combined his administrative and playing flair in the drawing-up of rules for the game in Trinity in 1868. Irish schools which had begun to be swept by the games' fever sweeping England formed teams to challenge the Trinity Second XV.

In the north of the country, rugby was built upon the success which cricket had already established. The North of Ireland Cricket Club allowed part of their grounds to be converted into a rugby pitch in 1868 and members of the cricket club formed the first team and committee. Match opponents came from the newly formed rugby club at Queen's University and the teams' first encounter is reported to have lasted three days. Inter-club matches between the newly formed clubs around Ireland were

Previous page: Cycling event at the Royal Dublin Society. Events there usually attracted competitors from overseas. The World Championship was won by Harry Reynolds from County Dublin in Denmark in 1896.

Above: Competitors line up for a sprint. Only one athlete has adopted the more modern stance in readiness for the 'off'.

Opposite: The first cup ever presented for rugby in the world. Sir Patrick Dun's Hospital Team, 1884.

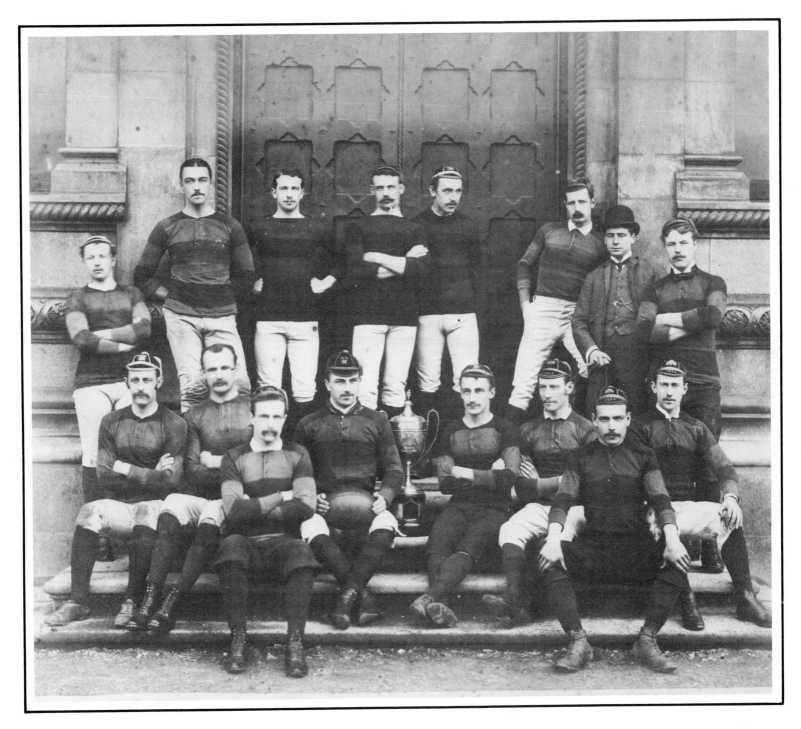

played and soon there was a desire for games at international level. To do this however the Irish clubs had to acquiesce to England's insistence on the formation of an Irish administrative body. In response, the major clubs met in December 1874 and the Irish Football Union was born. George Stack captained the Irish side at the first international at Kennington Oval in February 1875 and Irish rugby came of age.

One of the Dublin schools in which rugby was fostered was Cusack's Academy – the principal Michael Cusack had been one of Blackrock College's star rugby coaches. Conscious of the view of the role of sport in the moulding of youth, and at the same time disturbed at what he felt was the elitist and growing English domination of sport in Ireland, he established a native Irish response to the movement. Many of the ideas and attitudes associated with the development of organised sport in England found echoing chords here. The 'walk and talk' activity of English boys which proved so irritating to Victorian England was soon to be discouraged here also:

I remember the great change that came over the country . . . the young men in their idle hours loitered in dull fashion by the street and fence corners. In a few months how different things became! The country was soon humming with interest and activity, the ambitions of the young men were aroused . . . prepared to do or die for the honour of the little village.

Puirseal, P. The GAA in its time. *The Purcell Family, Dublin, 1892.*

Left: Northern Ireland was the birthplace of Irish soccer, the IFA being founded in Belfast in 1880. As the game spread in popularity, clubs affiliated to the northern body. Following 1921, the Football Association of Ireland was founded for southern teams, their first international being played in Paris, 1924.

Opposite: The weight of the shot at sixteen pounds, later accepted as a worldwide standard, was first established at Trinity College in 1860.

As in England, the muscular christians were being formed here, so much so that when an Irish team arrived in New York in 1888 they were described as:

A (more) splendid assemblage of specimens of manhood would be difficult to find ... than the half-hundred clear complexioned and clean-limbed, stalwart, bright-eyed muscular, strapping and fine-looking young fellows grouped on the deck of the steamship Washington ... They were literally the flower of Erin's manhood.

Left: Steeple-chasing began in Ireland in Buttevant, County Cork, in 1752. The scales on the right were the jockey's weigh-in point and the inevitable bookmaker is poised ready for trade.

Above: Lisfannon Golf Course, Buncrana, County Donegal, founded in 1890. One year later Ireland was to establish its Golfing Union.

Opposite: Hurling on the beach at Red Bay, County Antrim.

Sport's extension to nationalism found even more willing echoes in Ireland than in England's public schools. Archbishop Croke, whom the newly formed Gaelic Athletic Association invited as Patron in 1884, responded in a letter which was almost to become the GAA's charter:

If we continue travelling for the next score years in the same direction that we have taken for some time past, condemning the sports that were practised by our forefathers, effacing our national features as though we were ashamed of them, and putting on, with England's stuff and broadcloths, her masher habits and other effeminate follies as she may recommend, we had better at once, and publicly, abjure our nationality, clap hands for joy at the sight of the Union Jack, and place 'England's bloody red' exultantly above 'the green'.

The military expression of that nationalism, which in England found voice in colleges' volunteer corps had a stormy parallel in Ireland. It seems almost certain that members of the Irish Republican Brotherhood formed the core of the association executive. This development was strenuously resisted by the priests of the country in whose

Henry Dunlop, marked his retirement from active involvement in sport by founding the Irish Champion Athletic Club in 1872. The club held competitions in amateur athletics and the first athletic titles were competed for in 1873. Initially competitions were confined, as they had been at Trinity and other athletic clubs, to people of 'genteel' origins, 'mechanics, artisans and labourers' being excluded. After much newspaper correspondence, however the 'genteel' criterion was modified to include those who could satisfy the management as to their 'respectability'. However, although Ireland held a long tradition in athletics (triple jump and hammer-throwing being Irish creations), no national governing body existed to regulate the sport until the GAA applied itself to the task in 1884. They

parishes new clubs had been established nationwide. As a consequence the GAA was to remain in the doldrums until the turn of the century when a new executive began an expansion campaign.

Other sports in Ireland, in particular athletics and cycling, were not to remain uninfluenced by the establishment of the Gaelic Athletic Association. A Trinity graduate,

Opposite: Play at Fitzwilliam, home of Irish tennis. Here in 1879, the first Irish Open Championships were held, with the Ladies' Open being held the same year.

Right: After the Gordon Bennett International Trophy road race in Ireland in 1903, attended by an international crowd of 100,000, the British Parliament passed a bill permitting roads to be closed for similar events.

promptly banned from their athletic competitions athletes who competed in events other than those organised by the GAA. All existing athletic and cycling clubs in the country met to plan their response to this ban, and E.J. Macredy of Trinity urged them to 'quash the Gaelic Union'. He believed the GAA to be only interested in developing hurling and that the organisation was political in origin. A war of words continued until in 1885 Dr Croke insisted on the ban's removal, a request which Michael Cusack somewhat grudgingly bowed to. Athletics received a great boost from this development and in Cork in 1886 both

organisations finally met in competition.

It has been said of the emphasis on sport in Victorian times that if earlier approaches to education had tried to make boys into men too soon, that the reverse became true and Victorians failed to make boys into men at all. Whichever approach one agrees with, there can be no doubt that almost all modern sports were nurtured, popularised and codified by Victorians' energies. It is to them modern sports enthusiasts owe their thanks.

CHAPTER NINE

The Empire

The massive jubilant crowds which welcomed Queen Victoria on her visits to Ireland dispelled any doubts there may have been regarding the secure and willing place held by the Irish in the British Empire. The Queen's first visit here was to a country just emerging from Famine in 1849 and she returned to open the Great Industrial Exhibition on Leinster Lawn in 1851. When Victoria and Albert visited again in 1861 they travelled beyond Dublin to Killarney and also to the Curragh where the Prince of Wales was camping with the troops.

Queen Victoria became a recluse from almost all her subjects after the death of Prince Albert and her prolonged mourning was not broken for the people of Ireland, at least until 1900, a year before her death. While this final visit had all the trimmings of a state occasion, the frail and elderly Queen did not elicit as much excitement as the younger, more attractive, figure had done.

Although Ireland was generally *en fête* for royal occasions, the welcome was not always unanimous. When the Land War and Home Rule campaign were in full swing during the heated 1880s, Dublin Corporation boycotted visits by the Prince of Wales and ignored the Golden Jubilee of Queen Victoria's coronation. During Victoria's last visit to Ireland in 1900, James Connolly and Maud Gonne co-operated in organising counter-demonstrations: a lantern slide display of British atrocities committed against the Boers in South Africa, and a children's picnic to detract

from the official one organised to honour the royal visit.

On the whole, however, the welcome was tumultuous, and allegiance unquestioned. Dublin was thoroughly illuminated for the occasion of Queen Victoria's Golden Jubilee in 1887 and all public offices closed for the holiday despite the Corporation boycott. And when Edward and Alexandra ascended the throne, their subsequent visits in 1903 and 1907 had perhaps the greatest impact of all, encouraged by their relative youth and Alexandra's beauty – all advertised by the increased use of photography.

While visiting the west of Ireland to review the work of the Congested Districts Board, the King and Queen were brought into contact with thousands of ordinary people. So moved was the population of the west that when old age pensions were introduced some years later, many old people there thought their five shillings per week was a direct result of the King himself having witnessed their poverty. For most Irish of the time, Irish nationalism and respect for and loyalty to the British monarchy were not exclusive. Many Home Rule supporters who had initially vowed to boycott official receptions to welcome Edward and Alexandra to the west subsequently changed their minds. A scramble often ensued to secure last-minute invitations for undoubted nationalists to meet the royal couple.

It could be argued that much of the loyalty to the British throne was economically based. Thousands volunteered to join the British army; throughout the nineteenth century

almost twice as many Irish soldiers proportionate to population joined the army as did men from England, Scotland and Wales. Ordinary recruits were drawn from the poorest sections of the Irish population, many being servants or agricultural labourers. Earnings were higher and more secure than those in unskilled work and pensions were generous for relatively short service. After fourteen years' service a man could retire with a pension for life and a lump sum of £21.

Even after retirement, the army continued to look after the interests of its soldiers. Each regiment had an employment register of jobs for ex-soldiers and several secure employers reserved positions for army men. In the early 1900s the Irish railways reserved six hundred jobs each year

for ex-soldiers and the Dublin Metropolitan Police and Royal Irish Constabulary admitted former soldiers on preferential terms. Even when a man fell on hard times, army charities existed to look after the ex-soldier or his widow and children; the Hibernian School in Dublin's Phoenix Park, for example, was established to educate orphans of Irishmen who died fighting in the Crimean War. Consequently, for most Irish soldiers, the British army was not viewed as a foreign army nor was it felt to contradict with a soldier's Irish identity. Indeed, for many it was the only alternative to emigration and enlistment rose when recession in Britain or the United States cut off that option.

As with individuals, entire towns depended on the

Previous page: Royal Irish Regiment, 1st Batallion, Egypt 1915. Training was undertaken here for Irish troops in preparation for the Gallipoli campaign.
Opposite: Strabane 1911. Parades to celebrate the coronation of King George V were held in many Irish towns.
Left: Loyal subjects welcome Edward VII on his visit to the west.
Below: A salute for the Viceroy, Lord Aberdeen, and his wife, while they were o. an inspection tour for the Congested Districts Board.

British army for their very existence. Up to forty towns in Ireland had some military presence and the financial input to each town was enormous. Shopkeepers in Fermoy, County Cork, earned £30,000 per month from military spending and the army provided the small town of Buttevant, County Cork, with 120 highly-valued civilian jobs.

The army officers were drawn from the Anglo-Irish gentry and, once commissioned, an officer would find his background had equipped him well for his role. Mornings were usually devoted to military duties such as parades and inspections, although this was often left to the NCO to undertake. Afternoons and evenings were free for sport and social engagements; officers played polo and shot, and several hunted three days a week in season. If posted to the Curragh, Dublin and its host of social engagements could be enjoyed while staying at the Kildare Street Club. Because of their religion and social standing, officers were in great demand for occasions such as country house parties, dinners and levees at Dublin Castle.

At the Castle, the Lord Lieutenant, the monarch's viceroy in Ireland, presided at the peak of the administrative hierarchy. Most lords lieutenant were rich and titled, and indeed such wealth was needed as they were expected to entertain regally. Debutantes were presented at the Castle and the Lord and Lady Lieutenant presided over court levees and performed ceremonial functions. They also hosted the highlight of the Irish social season, the St Patrick's Day Ball. Invitations were issued to as many titled people as could be mustered, Anglo-Irish gentry, army officers and senior civil servants.

The lords lieutenant and their wives did not confine all their energies to glittering Castle soirées, however. The Countess of Dudley was responsible for the establishment of a public health nursing scheme designed to improve hygiene and provide health education generally in the homes of the poor. Lord and Lady Aberdeen attempted large scale social improvements on their second appoint-

Opposite: Royal Irish Rifles arrive at Springfontein to fight in the Boer War. From both economic necessity and loyalty, Irishmen were willing volunteers for the army.

Right: Alexandra, Princess of Wales, welcomed on her visit to a convent. On such visits to Ireland, institutions were willing and anxious to obtain the royal seal of approval for their work.

Left: Clemance Brophy, 34th Regiment, wounded in the trenches, August 31st, 1855, in the Crimea. His chest and shoulder blade have been broken away and his arm shot off. Seen by Queen Victoria at Chatham.

Below: Christmas tea in the Gallery of the Royal Hospital Dublin for the boys of the Hibernian School and Drummond Institute, December 1903. The Hibernian School catered for boys whose fathers had been killed fighting the Boer War. They themselves were destined to fight in the First World War. Few would have survived.

Opposite: The Cotillon at the Flower Ball, St Patrick's Hall, Dublin Castle, 1902.

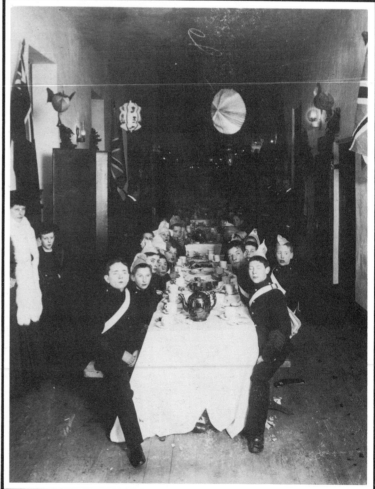

ment to the office in 1906. Lady Aberdeen, from whom most of the initiatives came, was a woman of wide interests and concern; chief among these being health. She established the Women's National Health Association, which was run by women for women. Clinics for babies were opened, as were playgrounds in slum areas; health visitors were employed and education campaigns in food and hygiene undertaken. As dirty milk infested with tuberculosis and scarlet fever was known to be a major

Left: Lord and Lady Aberdeen visiting the islands in Galway in their work for the Congested Districts Board. The development of the fish exporting industry was one of their main concerns in the west.

Below: An Irish welcome for visiting royalty. Few perceived a conflict between being Irish and being loyal subjects of the British Empire.

Opposite: Bank of Ireland, Dublin. Jubilant throngs gather to greet King George V and Alexandra, Princess of Wales, on the occasion of their visit to celebrate his coronation.

cause of infant death, Lady Aberdeen set up depots to provide the first supplies of sterilised milk in the city.

Not content with her trojan efforts in the field of public health, the country's First Lady also attempted economic enterprises. A passionate supporter of Home Rule, she understood the need for the development of native Irish industry and craft, and encouraged the making of lace and tweed products. Guests at Castle balls were to be dressed in a guaranteed Irish costume, which must have surprised Dublin society – but Lady Aberdeen was adamant.

But the tide of influence was slowly changing. Improved education and social mobility in Ireland meant that administrative positions in Dublin Castle soon were to be filled with native Irish for the first time. Social unrest would erupt in Dublin in the General Strike of 1913. A new era was dawning for Ireland as the sun set on this corner of the Empire.

Opposite: The Duke and Duchess of York (late King George V and Queen Mary) driving through Dublin, August 18th 1897.

Above: Lady Aberdeen with children of the Dublin tenements in one of the Ormond playgrounds founded by her. The wives of the Viceroys played a major role in the establishment of services for the poor in Ireland.

Right: Lady Aberdeen and the caravan which was to take health education to the masses. The war she waged on tuberculosis earned her the title 'Vice-Regal Microbe' from Arthur Griffith.

CHAPTER TEN

Behind the Camera

Photography can be said to be truly Victorian having been invented in 1839, two years after Queen Victoria was crowned. Credit for the first published invention of photography goes to Monsieur Daguerre, of France. So important was his invention that the French government bought out his patent for a lump sum and an annual pension. Thus, the process became freely available in France, while remaining under licence in Britain.

The daguerrotype as it is now called, was a positive process whereby a sheet of copper coated with silver nitrate gave a very high-definition photograph. Its main disadvantage was that it could not be copied and was a once-only photograph. At the same time in England, Fox Talbot, a country gentleman, was working on the same invention. When the news of Daguerre's patent reached him he quickly responded by registering his own process. Unlike Daguerre's, Fox Talbot's invention was a negative process using very thin sheets of paper covered in salts. When the photograph was taken off, a negative impression remained which could then be printed. The main advantage of this process was, of course, the ability to make copies. While the quality was not as high as that of Daguerre's and the exposure times lengthy, Fox Talbot's process did provide a negative.

The first practitioners of the new photography in Ireland established daguerrotype studios. Advertisements appeared in the newspapers inviting people to have their image taken in studios which were invariably at the top of tall buildings, to allow the maximum light for the procedure. The earliest surviving photographs of importance were taken by the Reverend Calvert Jones who had been taught the craft by Fox Talbot himself. Reverend Jones was on the Grand Tour of Europe when he stopped off in Dublin and left to us thirty-six views of Ireland. Originally it was thought that only twelve to fourteen of his views remained until research for this book revealed the remainder. Both soldiers, who were used to standing still, and buildings were popular choices as subjects for Fox Talbot's long exposure time, and indeed the Reverend Jones' legacy to us are photographs of Powerscourt House, Trinity College and other outstanding buildings of the city.

By the time of the Famine, photography was already 10 years old, but unfortunately there are no known surviving photographs. One possible explanation for this is that the process was still too cumbersome and slow for it to be used in more remote areas; another is that the potential value of photographic journalism had yet to be realised. The first attempt at connecting a picture to current news in Ireland

was after the Young Irelanders' 1848 rebellion. William Smith O'Brien was photographed in Kilmainham Jail alongside a soldier, the Governor and Francis Meagher, and the photographs subsequently sold in Dublin's shops. Indeed, counterfeits were also on sale with actors posing as the original group in the jail. Had the next photographic development, the wet plate process, been available during Famine times, it is possible that we might today have pictures to evoke that era of our history. The wet plate process did not come to Ireland until the early 1850s and it scored high by having reduced exposure times to seconds and by using glass plates which gave high definition negatives.

The gentry of Ireland were first to adopt the new invention as a hobby. Two of the greatest exponents of the craft were Lady Ross and the Honourable Augusta Crofton. Their photographs are fine examples of early photography but as their lives were fairly restricted within their estates, it is from this milieu that their subjects are drawn and it was

Opposite top: Perhaps the first surviving photographs of the west of Ireland, taken in Donegal by Derryman James Glass, c.1860. A professional photographer, he practised his craft on his walking tours. A haversack on his back, weighing almost two stone, contained glass jars full of chemicals, portable dark room, glass plates, tripod and a large unwieldly camera. Some photographers of the Wet Plate era pushed their gear around on a handcart!

Opposite left: Probably the earliest photograph (c.1860) of an Irish person at work on the canal at Clonmel left to us by an enthusiastic amateur. Dr William Despard Hamphill (from Clonmel) was awarded a medal at the Paris Exhibition for his photographs of local scenery.

Right: William Smith O'Brien (seated) and Francis Meagher to his right, in Kilmainham Jail, 1848. The prison governor holds the key. An enormous demand existed for photographs of condemned prisoners and often the unscrupulous had actors pose for the picture.

Above: Augusta Crofton with camera, a present from Dad from the Great Exhibition in London, 1852. Photography was considered a lady-like pursuit.

to be left to others at a later date to record life throughout the country. The forerunner to the postcard industry developed around the same time in Ireland; photographs of the Giants' Causeway, Killarney and other beauty spots were being put on sale for the growing tourist industry. Thus, our biggest collection of photographs of Ireland in the latter part of the nineteenth century is from the commercial photographer. The greatest section of these comes from William Lawrence. William's mother owned a toy shop in O'Connell Street, Dublin, on the site of the present Madame Nora's. When William inherited the business he opened a small photographic studio at the rere of the premises. Seeing that opportunity lay in commercial-views photography he fully developed this aspect of his business. Although not a photographer himself, he employed a team of photographers, the best known of these being Robert French who had been a member of the Royal Irish

Left: Enthusiast at work. With the invention of the wet plate process and the first flush of enthusiasm for the latest hobby, amateurs formed hobby clubs, the earliest being the Dublin Photographic Society in 1854. The hobby however declined until the Rev Maddocks' invention of the dry plate process rejuvenated both the hobby and the Photographic Society of Ireland.

Right: From the Lawrence Collection, a view of Broad Street, Charleville, County Cork. Few towns were unvisited by Lawrence's roving staff – often Robert French. During the 1890s Lawrence published illustrated guides to Ireland and began postcard publication at the beginning of this century.

Constabulary before joining Lawrence. The Lawrence company, and in particular Robert French, left us over 40,000 views of Ireland, an invaluable heritage which is housed in the National Library.

A major development in photography was contributed by the Reverend Maddocks who discovered that by combining gelatine on glass with other chemicals, a dry, rather than a wet, plate resulted. No longer would photographers need to haul around soggy chemicals and endure the mess they created. For the first time, photography was portable. Not only that; the dry plate lasted much longer than the wet, which allowed time to send the plate away to a photographic supplier without having to be involved in the developing process oneself. This innovation really opened up photography as new enthusiasts did not need to be technically-minded, not only was it portable, it was simple. Access to photography became more common,

hobby clubs and societies sprang up and our pictorial records of life in Ireland begin to bulge from the early 1890s.

Ireland's only claim to fame in the active development of photography came from Professor Joly of Trinity College, Dublin, who invented the first practical colour photograph by using a line system very much like that used in colour television. Unfortunately, at the same time in Chicago, a James McDonagh claimed to have invented the same system; he patented it in 1892. A court case subsequently took place in the United States to decide ownership of the claim. Professor Joly was unable to attend and he lost the case, afterwards becoming a broken man. However, in any international record of photography Ireland's only inclusion is that of Professor Joly.

The 1890s also brought the invention of the print photograph in newspapers, and for the first time the

127

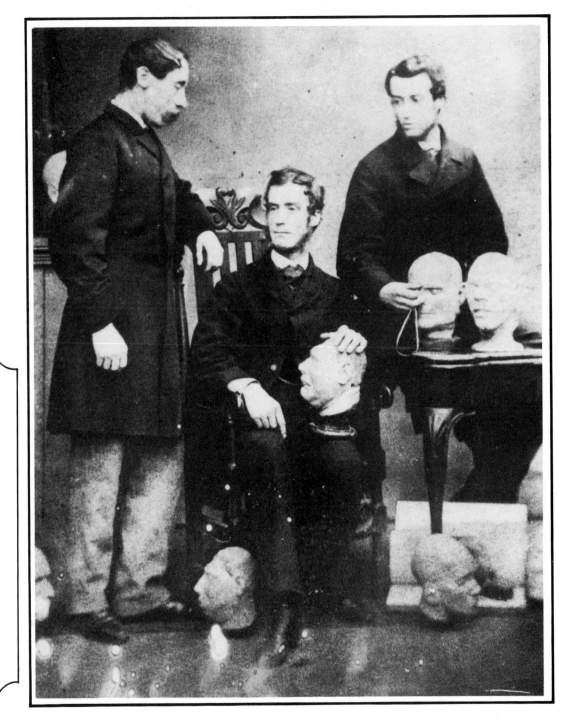

Opposite: Perhaps the first chronicler to record women's lives, Rose Shaw was governess to the Gledstanes family, Clogher, County Tyrone. She travelled the Clogher Valley recording the peasants' way of life and developed her photographs, worthy of both technical and artistic merit, in the windowless silver storage room at the Gledstanes home.

Right: Professor Leon Gluckman, a Hungarian immigrant who operated a Daguerre portrait studio in Sackville Street, Dublin, during the 1840s. It was fashionable in Dublin to have one's portrait taken, and later almost essential for one's photograph to appear on visiting cards.

common man was able to daily enjoy the fruits of photography. The first staff newspaper photographer was probably Tom Barker of *The Cork Examiner* who has left us a superb record of Cork. Another photographer from Cork was Joseph Cashman, who while working in Dublin photographed the 1913 strike and later the rebellion in 1916.

Pictures have an ability to communicate in a way that words can never achieve. News photographs, cinema and then television have been used since the last century to highlight injustice and inequality and to champion causes. Today, to have access to pictures of African famine is almost commonplace, but it was surely an inspired move on the part of those who first allied the photograph to the cause. As successive famines and continued hardship were suffered by those in the west of Ireland, those pressing for development there presented a portfolio of pictures which graphically portrayed the reality of the situation to the Mansion House Committee of Inquiry into the congested districts. And not only did the Royal Commission of Enquiry send inspectors into Dublin's slums to investigate the living conditions of the working class, photographers also went to bring back indisputable proof that many of the city's inhabitants did live in incredible squalour.

Then almost as soon as photography had shown a more serious side to its versatility, it was to be overshadowed: the flickering moving pictures of the Lumière brothers were soon to be seen in Ireland.

Left: John Gough of Eustace Street, Dublin, sold pictures of current events and portrait photographs of popular figures such as Queen Victoria. The poster, lower right, advertises the precursor of the postcard industry.

Opposite: A children's outing from Cork, c.1911. Taken by the craftsman Tom Barker of *The Cork Examiner,* this is an outstanding photograph despite the absence of modern technology. Without the benefit of today's motor driven camera Tom Barker had only one chance to record this event. He achieved, in a fraction of a second, the centre in exact focus with the less important area out of focus, giving perfect composition.

Illustration Sources

The photographs in this book were selected from the huge collection gathered to produce the RTE TV series 'Shadows of Ourselves'.

Below are listed the sources for the pictures that are printed in this book:

British Army Museum 111, 206; Eddie Chandler 31, 81, 125, 126 left, 129, 130; Civic Museum, Dublin 44, 85, 89, 12 bottom right; Ian Cairnduff 103; John Cooney 20; Cork Examiner 43, 58, 94, 96, 105, 131; Dept. of Irish Folklore, UCD 15, 19 left; Caoimhin Ó Danachair 48 left, 57, 98 top; Lord Dudley 60, 61 left, 91, 113 left; Daniel Gillman 26 bottom, 63, 65 top, 73, 75, 76, 79, 82, 87, 92, 108 left; Arthur Guinness, Dublin 11; Tom Hayden 6; Paddy Healy 83; Magee University, Derry 56; Matt McNulty 108 right; National Library of Ireland 10, 12 top left, 13, 22 top right, 37, 47, 54 right, 69, 70, 98 bottom, 106 right, 127, (Clonbrock Collection) 29, 30, 32, 33, 34, 35, 38, 39, 59 top, 96; National Museum 17, 19 right, 20 bottom, 21, 26 top, 45 left, 84, 85, 93; National Science Museum, London 123; Larry O'Connor 25 right, 42 right; Private collection 42 left; Public Records Office, Belfast 2, 59 bottom; Royal Society of Antiquaries of Ireland 64, 65 bottom, 66, 67, 68, 88 left, 101; RTE (Murtagh Collection) 77 top, 115, 119; Royal Archives, Windsor 8, 116, 117, 118 bottom, 119; Scottish National Trust 3, 20 top, 22 left, 61 right, 71, 72, 78, 80 (Aberdeen Collection), 81, 90, 99, 113 right, 118 top, 121; Shankill Road Mission, Belfast 95; Rose Shaw Collection 49; Dublin University, TCD 124 bottom; Ulster Museum 1, 45 right, 46, 48 right, 51, 97, 107, 112; Ulster Folk and Transport Museum 9, 16, 18, 24, 25, 88 right, 124 top, 126 right, 128, (Green Collection) 41, 50 left; Wynne Collection 27, 50 right, 53, 54 left, 55, 77 bottom, 78, 102, 104, 106 left.

The author thanks all those who provided photographs and gave advice, especially Daniel Gillman and Ita Wynne.

In addition to the list above, the author thanks the following who helped in many ways, especially with research and advice on illustrations: Belfast City Library, S. Cleary, Michael Corcoran, Seamus Deval, Mr & Mrs Luke Dillon-Mahon, F.E. Dixon, Dublin Port and Docks Board, G.A. Duncan, H. Eustace, Irish Architectural Archive, Tom Kenny, Linenhall Library, Peamount Hospital, Peter Pearson, Royal Dublin Society, and Eugene Hogan and Martin Ryan, both of the National Library of Ireland.